How to cope with my partner leaving

Janet Haines
Mandy Matthewson

Acknowledgements:
Steven Haines
Robyn Cartledge
Coverart designed by Freepik
(www.freepik.com)

This workbook offers suggestions on how to cope after your partner leaves the relationship. We do not guarantee that these suggested strategies will resolve all psychological symptoms. You may wish to seek alternative assistance from a mental health professional.

How to cope with my partner leaving
Janet Haines & Mandy Matthewson
Copyright © 2025
ISBN: 978-1-923573-15-4

About the authors

Dr Janet Haines has a PhD in Clinical Psychology and has worked as an academic and researcher for 17 years, and in private practice for 30 years helping people facing life problems.

Dr Mandy Matthewson is a Clinical Psychologist, educator and researcher with more than two decades of experience supporting people through life's toughest challenges.

For B who discovered that life didn't end when his partner left,
it was the beginning of a life that was better than he'd imagined

Table of contents

Table of contents 5
Introduction 7
A major stressful life event 8
    Why is a relationship breakdown a major stressful life events? 8
    What to expect from a major stressful life event 9
The notion of a life crisis 10
    How do we react to a life crisis? 10
Is it normal to feel like this? 14
Grieving the losses you experience 15
    What is grief? 15
Why do I feel so frightened? 20
    What is my nervous system doing? 20
How will I cope? 24
    Coping 24
    Problem-focused coping vs. emotion-focused coping 24
    Problem-approach vs. problem-avoidance coping 25
    Identifying your preferred coping style 28
Why is my partner behaving like this? 32
    What does my former partner's behaviour say about our lives together? 32
    But why are they being so unfeeling? 33
The influence of attachment 35
What can I do to feel better? 36
Controlling your sympathetic nervous system 38
    Range of arousal 38
    Anxiety management strategies 39
    Breathing and heart rate 40
    Breathing and muscle tension exercises 41
    Quieting your mind 47
Dealing with sleep disturbance 52
    What can I do about my sleep problems? 54
Regulating your emotions 56
    Recognising and dealing with your emotions 57
    The link between your emotions and your behaviour 61

- Managing your anger 65
  - Exit and wait strategy 65
  - Controlling thoughts that trigger anger 66
- Learning acceptance 70
  - A change of attitude 70
- Using effective coping strategies 73
  - Building your coping repertoire 73
- Thinking your way to less distress 83
  - How are our thoughts affected? 83
  - Core beliefs 84
  - Cognitive errors 84
  - Why do we think in unhelpful ways? 95
  - Underlying assumptions of logical errors 97
  - Understanding automatic thoughts 100
  - Catching automatic thoughts 100
  - Understanding and noticing logical errors 102
  - Reframing your thoughts (cognitive restructuring) 104
  - Making the restructured thinking habitual 109
  - Targeting the assumptions 109
- Assertive communication 113
  - Asking for change 113
  - Negotiating for what you want 116
- Improving the quality of your life 118
  - Values clarification exercise for choosing preferred activities 118
- Looking after yourself 121
- Additional reading 122

Introduction

This workbook has been produced to try to help you cope in the immediate aftermath of your romantic/intimate relationship ending. It is focused on that initial period of time when everything seems so terrible, chaotic and out of control. It will try to help you through that period of time when you have no idea what to do and when you feel like you will not be able to recover. It will try to set you on a pathway to recovery, moving towards a future full of opportunities… even if that does not seem possible right now.

We understand that the breakdown of an important relationship is an individual experience for people that is not identical to the experiences of others. The circumstances that lead up to the breakdown can be complicated and painfully drawn out or can be sudden and shocking, seemingly happening out of the blue. This workbook is for people who find the experience of a relationship breakdown distressing, no matter the circumstances or context of the end of the relationship.

The content of this workbook is quite straightforward. It provides you with an explanation of what is happening and why you are reacting in the way you are experiencing. It then provides you with some means to feel better in the short-term. It does not give you a complete understanding of the complexities of relationships and their end but it is a guide to getting through a difficult time in your life.

A major stressful life event

First, you probably need to put what is happening in the context of other life events you may have experienced. The loss of an important relationship is usually considered to be a major stressful life event. What does this mean? A major stressful life event is something that happens to a person that causes them to feel distress and that has a significant impact on their life and wellbeing.

Not all events in your life that stress you would be considered major stressful life events. Getting a speeding ticket is stressful, but it is not a major stressful life event. The same goes for losing your credit card, having an argument with your sister, or having to replace your burst hot water cylinder. All of these things require that you do something to fix the problem, but they are the sort of difficulties you will get stressed about and then recover from as soon as they are over.

At the opposite end of the stress scale from major stressful life events are what are termed daily hassles. These are the irritating sorts of things that may cause a stressful twinge but do not really have a greater impact on you than a brief period of annoyance or stress. These would be things like getting a parking ticket, forgetting to pay the electricity bill, getting a flat tyre on your car, or missing the bus.

Why is a relationship breakdown a major stressful life events?

When researchers first started thinking about how events in our lives differ in terms of how distressing they are, they got people to rate various events in terms of how stressful they were considered to be and how much of an impact they had on a person's life. In this way, the most severe of the major stressful life events were those that were rated as the most stressful and had the biggest impact.

When we looked at the major life events that cause the greatest stress and have the biggest impact, among the more stressful events were:

    Death of a spouse or death of your child

    Divorce

    Marital/relationship separation

    Death of a close family member other than a spouse or your child

    Imprisonment.

So, you can see that the breakdown of an important romantic relationship is understood to be one of the most stressful experiences with which a person has to cope. It is probably also worth noting that, often, the breakdown of a relationship causes a range of other problem situations to develop. These might include financial stressors, accommodation stressors, dealing with the legal system, losing friendships, etc. Stressful life events have been demonstrated to have more of an impact when more than one event occurs at once. The stressful nature of the experiences is cumulative.

It should also be kept in mind that some people will cope with a relationship breakdown without experiencing undue distress. This is likely due to the fact that the relationship was not really meeting their needs and its loss has less of an impact on them. Of course, for these people, the lack of distress would mean they would be unlikely to seek out ways to manage the situation.

For those people who do experience distress, this is due to the relationship being a major stressful life event for you. It is worth keeping in mind that many people experience relationship breakdowns in this way. What you are feeling is a normal reaction to a very stressful thing happening in your life.

What to expect from a major stressful life event

As a result of the severe nature of a major stressful life event, we should have an expectation that we are in for a difficult time when they occur. And that is true when an important relationship breaks down. You will be facing a challenging time for a while, and then you will move on to a new phase of your life… even if you do not believe that at this moment.

The notion of a life crisis

This idea that you are in for a difficult time but that you will reach a point where you will be able to move on with life fits with what we know about how people cope with a crisis in their life. Psychologists have investigated how people cope with crises in their life and found that there are similarities between individuals with regard to the processes associated with reactions to these crises.

How do we react to a life crisis?

As we go through life, most of us face challenging times. We have learned how people react to these experiences. Although people are individuals and the way we cope with difficult times may differ to some degree, there does seem to be an underlying structure to how we cope with crises in our lives.

We react to the shocking nature of the crisis

When we first learn of these types of crises, we tend to go into a shocked state. Although we understand something bad has happened, we tend to feel like the events are unreal. That sense of unreality can be explained.

The pressure that is placed on us at these times triggers a chemical reaction in our brains that functions to protect us from the enormity of what has occurred. Your brain sorts out quickly that you need to do what is necessary to get by so this chemical process protects you from the full emotional impact in those early stages. This process can result in a specific feeling or reaction called dissociation. It commonly occurs when we are put under intense pressure.

Despite the experience of dissociation being helpful, protecting you from the full emotional impact of what you have experienced until you are in a better position to cope, the feeling can be uncomfortable. You will feel disengaged from events around you, and it is harder to make sense of things and process complex information about what has occurred and what you need to do. It is best to understand this state as your brain putting you in survival mode. You will be able to handle the things you need to do to get by, but you will feel disengaged and distant from what has happened. This is caused by a neuro-chemical reaction.

This feeling can last for a short period or for days. Also, you can move in and out of this state as new aspects of your crisis become apparent. With each stressful thing, your brain will put you back in that state that is self-protective but is uncomfortable and can be unpleasant.

The idea when you are in this state is to not put undue pressure on yourself. When you are in that disengaged, dissociative state, it is not the time to make life-changing decisions or reach conclusions about what you have to do from here on. Remember that you are in survival mode and not capable of complex thinking about important matters. Also, know that this state will end, and you will have time to plan and make decisions after it has ended. Take advantage of this state. Remember that it occurs to protect you from the full emotional impact of the bad thing that has happened.

> *Helena's husband told her that he didn't want to be married to her anymore and said he was leaving. A stressful and distressing conversation took place, but, in the end, her husband packed a bag and left. She had no idea where he was going and what was going to happen next. Helena reached out to her family, and her two sisters came to her house to console her and support her in whatever way they were able. They asked her what they could do to help, but Helena didn't know what to say. She felt numb. It felt like she was looking down on herself, watching herself sit on the couch. Her face felt numb. Helena knew she felt bad but couldn't really say what it was she was thinking about. Thoughts seemed to come into her mind and then disappear. Her sisters were worried about Helena. She seemed so disengaged. They didn't want to leave her alone.*

We then go on an emotional roller coaster ride

When we come out of this shocked state, the full impact of the emotional cost of the experience is felt. After a period of feeling disengaged and unsettled, we then feel emotionally overwhelmed and emotionally out of control. It feels like we have no idea how we are going to feel from moment to moment. Feelings can change from intense despair to fearfulness to anger. Our emotions are volatile, and the immediate emotional state seems to be unrelated or not directly related to what is happening at that moment.

This will be a really difficult time for you. The intensity of the feelings you have will challenge your ability to cope at times. Unfortunately, this emotional roller coaster ride can continue for some time although the nature of your emotional response may change. For example, you may start feeling very sad or anxious and fearful. These feelings might give way to intense and overwhelming anger as time goes on.

This can be a challenging time. There is no way to avoid this emotional roller coaster ride. There is no magical thing you can do to skip this part of your reaction to what has happened to you. However, you may be able to do two things: (1) reduce the intensity of your feelings and bring them down to a more manageable level using techniques we will discuss later, and (2) shorten the duration of this stage of your reaction by using strategies focused on how you think about and cope with what is happening. We will talk about these later as well.

> *It had been two weeks since Helena's husband told her he was ending their marriage and had just left. Helena felt like she was going crazy. She couldn't control how she felt, and this had resulted in some embarrassing moments. For example, she burst into tears as she and her colleagues were leaving the room after a meeting. Although people were sympathetic, she felt that her colleagues would think she had gone mad. Helena felt her emotions had a mind of their own, and there wasn't anything she could do to control them. She was desperate to feel a bit more normal, but her mind was being bombarded by thoughts about her marriage and what she believed to be an uncertain future. She tried to distract herself, but this didn't help as much as she thought it would. Helena's sisters didn't know what to do with all her tears. They tried to comfort her and reassure her, but nothing seemed to help.*

We then enter a period of reflection

The emotional roller coaster ride will end. It will be exhausting and stretch your capacity to cope, but there will come a time when it is over. You will then start to reflect on what has happened and what it means. This period of reflection comes at a time when your emotional state is under control enough for you to be able to think more clearly about your life and your future.

This is an important part of the process of adjusting to what has happened. You have to try to make sense of what has happened. After coming out the other end of the emotional roller coaster ride, you will be in a better position to think clearly about the important aspects of your experience. You will be more able to adjust your views about what has happened and perhaps see it from a different point of view.

> *Helena had noticed that she hadn't been feeling as out of control emotionally as she had done previously. This was a relief. It also gave her a chance to start to think more clearly about what happened. She spent a lot of time thinking about her relationship with her husband. She thought about how her relationship had changed in recent times. She spent some time thinking about whether she had been truly happy towards the end of the relationship or whether she had just been drifting along without really thinking about whether the relationship was meeting her needs. She went back and forth in her mind about lots of issues. Some days, she would think one thing, and then she would change her mind. She was just trying to make sense of what had happened.*

We then reach a point where we can move on

> *When she thought about it, Helena realised she really hadn't thought about the breakdown of her marriage in some time. Days or weeks would go past without thinking about it. She found she was just getting on with life. She had been busy at work, but she had managed to find time to catch up with friends and do some fun things. She knew where she was situated financially and was making some plans for the future. She felt in control and self-sufficient. These were good feelings. Although there were times when she felt sad about the end of the relationship and times when she felt a bit lonely, Helena also liked the idea that she was the one who was going to decide things about her future.*

There will be people who will tell you that you will 'get over' what has happened. However, that is not what occurs. You will reach a point where you will have integrated your experience into what you know about life and your place in the world. You will become the new version of you who has had this happen to them. In that way, you will move forward a wiser person with greater life experience. You may look back at the difficult time with regret, wishing that things had worked out differently, but you will also be in a position to deal with the reality of the situation and move forward, living the next stage of your life.

In this way, you should avoid trying to fight to get back the old version of you. It is not possible, and it is not necessary. The new version of you can be happy and optimistic. The new version can be exciting, and you can look forward to a bright future. These things will be determined by you and not by what has happened to you. It is hard to imagine that might be the case when you are in the middle of the emotional difficulties that come with the breakdown of a relationship, but these things are the case whether or not you currently believe it is possible.

Is it normal to feel like this?

When you feel emotionally out of control, you tend to believe it cannot be normal to feel that way. From what we know about how people react to life crises, these strong emotions that you are feeling are a normal reaction to a stressful event. You are facing a difficult process of adjustment, during which you will experience complicated emotions, all of which will be intense.

It is also normal to want back what you have lost. You will yearn for things to go back to 'normal', to a time when you felt more in control and less threatened. It is difficult to imagine a future that is different from the one you had planned.

> *Douglas was mourning the loss of his relationship. It wasn't even really his wife he was missing because they had been drifting apart for some time before she decided to leave. It was more the loss of the family unit and the sense of stability that offered him. He thought often about all the things he had expected to happen in the future that now wouldn't occur. For example, he and his wife had always talked about travelling when they retired, but he supposed he wouldn't do that now. Even though he thought it was odd, he felt like he was grieving for the things he had wanted but now didn't have available to him. He felt he couldn't tell anyone about these feelings because he thought they would never understand.*

The loss you feel can trigger a grief reaction that is a normal reaction to that loss. Not only will you grieve the loss of what you had, but you can also grieve the loss of what you expected to have in the future.

Grieving the losses you experience

The end of your relationship can cause you to feel a sense of grief in at least two ways. Firstly, you can grieve the loss of the things you used to have but no longer have because your relationship is over. Secondly, you can experience a sense of grief in relation to the things you expected to have in the future that you now know are no longer available to you within that relationship. This might be related to expectations you had or plans you made for the things you were going to do.

Consider this example.

> *Georgia met and fell in love with Thomas. They married and were happy for a period of time. However, Thomas became increasingly discontented, not only with the marriage but with his life in general. He hated his job and didn't like the burden of a home loan, and the expectations he believed came with being married. He just wanted to be free to do the things he enjoyed. In the end, Thomas made the decision to leave the relationship. He resigned from his job, sold up his assets and took off to travel around and, in his words, 'experience life'.*
>
> *Georgia was heartbroken. She didn't want Thomas to be unhappy in their relationship, but she missed him and found it difficult to be without him. However, the thing that surprised her the most was the deep sense of loss she felt for things she didn't even have. In particular, earlier in their relationship, Georgia and Thomas often spoke about having children. They made plans for these children, plotting out a life for them. With this future no longer available to her, Georgia realised she was grieving its loss. She was grieving the loss of children she never had. The grief felt strong and real.*

Whatever the source of the grief, these challenges have the capacity to make you feel overwhelmed. They represent a challenge to you to rise to the demands of the situation and cope with your reaction to them.

What is grief?

Grief is a universally experienced emotional reaction in response to loss or perceived loss. Typically, it is experienced in relation to the loss of someone or something important to you.

Acute grief

Acute grief occurs immediately after the loss. These feelings of grief occur irrespective of the nature of the loss. This type of grief is associated with severe or intense feelings of distress.

> *Kayla felt like she couldn't take a deep breath in. She felt like she was going to tip over the edge and fall into a deep abyss. She didn't know how she was going to be able to cope with these feelings. She could not imagine surviving this emotional onslaught. Kayla's husband had left and he wasn't coming back. She was trying to make sense of what had happened. She had never felt this distressed before. It was overwhelming. No one could comfort her. The only person she wanted was her husband, who was gone. She couldn't bear to be around people, but she couldn't bear to be alone. Even being surrounded by people who cared about her did not ease the intense feeling of loneliness. The strength of her emotions made her feel panicked, and then she felt frightened by her panicky feelings. She couldn't see how this feeling would ever end. She longed for her husband.*

In the initial phases of acute grief, you can feel shock and numbness. You feel disengaged from what is happening. This dissociative experience is protective, in a sense, from the intensity of the emotional reactions. However, there will come a time when the full strength of your emotional reactions will be felt.

The emotional reactions to the loss you have experienced can be varied and may change over the course of the period of acute grief. It is well understood that grief is not only about feelings of sadness. It can be associated with a broad range of difficult emotional states including anger, regret, loneliness, emptiness, fear and guilt.

Let's consider an example.

> *Daniel always considered himself to be a pretty down-to-earth sort of person. He rarely got upset about things. He used to laugh and shake his head when people around him would become stressed over things he considered not worth his energy. He had assumed he would always be this way and always be able to cope. Then, his marriage ended, and his wife left him. Daniel was hit with a confusing array of emotions that he couldn't recall ever experiencing before. He had never realised he could experience such emotional turmoil. One minute, he was overwhelmed by sadness and feelings of longing for his wife to come back to him. Then he was angry with her. Then, he was frightened that these feelings would never go away. Then, the sadness would return in such a profound way that he didn't know how he would be able to cope with it.*

These emotional reactions have been described as the most painful that can be experienced by an individual. At the beginning, they may seem to be always present. However, before long, this changes and you experience the feelings of grief in bursts or waves. These waves of grief tend to be triggered by reminders of what has happened or things that make you think of the person you have lost.

> *Daniel would think for a moment that he was feeling better. However, he would then be hit with a wave of emotion so strong that it would take his breath away. This wave of grief would occur when there were obvious reminders of his wife and what had happened. Even the mention of his wife's name would be enough to trigger this overwhelming burst of distress. But it was also triggered by indirect reminders. When he got into his car, he was hit by a wave of distress because he remembered the last time he had been in the car with his wife. The unexpected nature of these reminders made it difficult for Daniel. He felt he couldn't predict how he was going to be feeling from one moment to the next. He felt that nothing was stable anymore.*

These waves of grief do lessen over time, both in terms of their frequency of occurrence and in their strength or intensity. This reduction will allow you to regain a feeling of emotional balance. At this time, your attention will be more focused on events outside of you rather than being focused on your emotional state.

> *Although there were times when the breath was knocked out of Daniel by the waves of grief he felt, he realised that these waves were not coming as frequently or lasting as long. He found himself being distracted by things such as work. In fact, it was a relief to be back at work because it allowed him to feel almost like his normal self for periods of time. He realised that when he stopped concentrating on other things, he would feel distressed again. So, Daniel liked to keep himself busy as much as he could.*

Integrated grief

Integrated grief is experienced after you transition beyond the acute grief stage. To reach a point of integrated grief may take you several months or more, or may occur sooner.

There are signs of you having reached integrated grief. For example, you can think about the person you have lost or what you have lost without the overwhelming nature of your earlier emotional responses. You can pick up your life again, returning to work and engaging in activities that give you pleasure.

> *Although he still strongly felt the loss of his wife and the end of his marriage, Daniel found he was able to do more of the things he would normally do to keep him busy. He was able to concentrate better at work. He started to meet up with friends and engage in social activities with them. Sometimes, he felt like he was in a strange place, somewhere between being upset and his more usual down-to-earth way of looking at the world. He wasn't quite sure where he should be between these two states, but he felt that he was moving in the right direction.*

It is often the case that you can move forward with a better perspective on life, a greater understanding of what is important in life, and a new focus on the things that matter. These positive changes in outlook have been identified to occur after a serious event in your life. The life event acts as a catalyst for you to change your outlook on life. It causes you to reprioritise things so that your focus is more on the important issues in your life and less on the more minor things that no longer seem to matter.

> *Although never a person to get upset about minor hassles, Daniel recognised that he was guilty of sometimes neglecting his important relationships when he was busy with his life. After his marriage ended, and now that he was feeling a bit better, Daniel was taking the time to pay attention to other important people in his life. It seemed like a natural thing to do. In fact, he thought that it wasn't even a really conscious decision on his part to treat his family and friends better. Instead, it was something he wanted to do, so it was no hardship for him to spend more time with the important people in his life.*

For most people, this is a point where you move on with your life, being the new person you have become as a result of the loss you have experienced. However, for a small number of people, this is more challenging to achieve. These individuals tend to stay in a state of acute grief. This prolonged grief reaction is known as complicated grief. However, complicated grief is not the typical outcome of a grieving process. Most people transition through to a point where they can experience life in a meaningful way.

Disenfranchised grief

One of the factors that can make grieving more difficult is when the grief you experience is disenfranchised. What does this mean? Disenfranchised grief is when your grief reaction does not fit with society's expectations. Our society has created certain expectations regarding how people grieve and about what they should grieve. When the trigger for your grief or the way in which you are grieving does not fit with those societal expectations, you can feel disenfranchised.

Disenfranchised grief can occur in numerous contexts. Importantly for our discussion here, your grief over a loss that is not death (e.g., the loss of a relationship), your grief for something that did not actually occur (e.g., loss of a future you hoped to have), or grief for the loss of a loved one from your life even though that person caused you distress, are all likely to disenfranchise your grief. In all of these cases, it is harder to obtain the same sort of sympathy and support that are received by people who are grieving a loss in more societally approved ways or because of experiences society sees as acceptable reasons for grieving.

Certainly, even though this is not true, disenfranchised grief is typically considered to be less important or less significant than more commonly accepted grief. As a result, you can experience disregard for your feelings. As a consequence of this disregard, you can be denied the right to mourn in the usual sense or in the way you would normally choose to mourn.

Of course, disenfranchised grief does not make the grief less real for you. The fact that others do not validate your feelings does not mean they are not legitimate. It may mean that you will need to seek other avenues for expressing your grief or other ways of seeking the help and support you need. Consider the following ways of helping you cope.

Table 1: Ways of coping with disenfranchised grief.

Seek out supportive people who understand what you are experiencing.   These might be people who have experienced a similar grief experience or they may be people who understand what you have lost and how important this loss is to you. They may also be people who have a more thorough understanding of your relationship so appreciate the value to you of aspects of the relationship you have lost.
Create a mourning ritual that is important to you.   Rituals are often important in the mourning process. In the absence of other means of expressing your grief, you may keep items that have a sentimental value. You may prepare an album of photographs of important events in your relationship. You might write a farewell letter to your ex-partner without any intention of ever sending it.
Ask for the help you need.   Without having to disclose the reasons why you are seeking assistance, you can still ask for help. Let your support network of family and friends know when you need company, when you need to be distracted by an activity, or when you need someone to listen to you talk.
Seek professional help.   When you need to discuss your grief in a non-judgmental environment, professional help can provide you with that opportunity. Seeking professional help can also assist you in normalising your grief so that you see it is a natural reaction to loss despite the rejection of this by others.

Why do I feel so frightened?

You are facing a situation that is outside your normal experience. Even if you have experienced other relationship breakdowns, they tend to be different in terms of their character and process. In any case, relationship breakdowns tend not to happen so frequently that they become part of your normal day-to-day life. It is not surprising that you would feel nervous about having to cope with such a difficult experience.

In general, people cope best when they feel that things are in their control. After the breakdown of a relationship, you are facing a period of uncertainty. You do not know what is going to happen, and there will be certain events that you feel might happen, and you may worry that you will not deal with them well. There can be fears about having to start over or fears about being alone forever. There can also be fears about your partner moving on without you. Our minds are capable of thinking up things we need to worry about.

> *Although Glen had never been much of a worrier, it seems he had turned into one since the end of his relationship. He worried during the day, and he lay awake at night worrying. He would worry about real things that were currently requiring his attention, such as, the negotiations he had to go through for the property settlement. But, he also worried about things that hadn't even happened. For example, he worried that if he met someone he liked, he did not know whether he should pursue a relationship with that person, or how that would work, or whether he ever wanted to get married again. He realised he was worrying about an imaginary person in a made up situation but he still couldn't stop. When he managed to stop worrying about one thing, he just started worrying about something else.*

In addition, there is a reason for feeling fear that is more fundamental and more related to how your nervous system reacts to stress. We have built in mechanisms that react when we are placed in threatening or stressful situations. It is worth taking a moment here to explain these mechanisms, because this will help you understand why you are reacting with anxiety and will help you understand the strategies you can use to help you feel better when we explain them to you.

What is my nervous system doing?

Your autonomic nervous system (ANS) is the part of your nervous system that drives your functioning. It regulates your heart rate and temperature and makes other adjustments that are required for you to function on a moment-by-moment basis.

Your ANS is divided into two parts: the parasympathetic nervous system and the sympathetic nervous system. Your parasympathetic nervous system is the part of your ANS that should be driving you most of the time. It makes sure everything is ticking along so that your body gets what it needs and you can function well.

Your sympathetic nervous system has a specialised function. It is your self-protection system that automatically activates when you are under threat. So, if you were crossing the road and a truck came screaming around the corner, your sympathetic nervous system would activate so that you could quickly and efficiently move out of the way of the truck and reach safety. Adrenaline would release into your system, causing your hands to shake and your heart rate to increase, but you would reach the safety of the footpath on the other side of the road, and you would be fine. Your brain would then recognise that you were safe, and your sympathetic nervous system would turn off, and your parasympathetic nervous system would take over again.

Your sympathetic nervous system is attuned to your brain perceiving signs of threat. It activates when you are at risk of harm and prepares you to deal with that threat. It is an effective self-protection system when you are under threat. Unfortunately, for people who develop an overly sensitive sympathetic nervous system or for people facing challenges in life, their sympathetic nervous system will activate at the slightest indication that something is wrong and will prepare them to deal with the threat. This can occur even when there really is no threat to manage. This is what happens when you are anxious in the absence of an obvious cause of your anxiety or an obvious sign of immediate danger. In effect, your brain cannot distinguish between an external threat (e.g., a truck coming around the corner) and an internal threat (e.g., you having worrying or anxiety-provoking thoughts). An overly sensitive nervous system will rely on its self-defence mechanism to protect you from perceived harm.

Your nervous system will react to crises in your life that do not present a threat of physical harm. Although the breakdown of a relationship is stressful, the breakdown itself is not physically threatening to you. Nevertheless, your sympathetic nervous system can be triggered by the breakdown. As stated, your brain cannot always distinguish between an external threat to your physical integrity and a threat to your emotional well-being that is caused by the way you think.

Below is a table providing an overview of the activities of the parasympathetic and sympathetic nervous systems.

Table 2: The functions of the parasympathetic and sympathetic nervous system.

	Parasympathetic	Sympathetic
Eyes	Constricts pupils	Dilates pupils
Salivary glands	Stimulates salivation	Inhibits salivation
Heart	Slows heartbeat	Accelerates heartbeat
Lungs	Constricts bronchi	Dilates bronchi
Stomach	Stimulates digestion	Inhibits digestion
Liver	Stimulates bile release	Simulates glucose release
Kidneys		Stimulates release of adrenaline and noradrenaline*
Intestines	Stimulates peristalsis and secretion	Inhibits peristalsis and secretion
Bladder	Contracts bladder	Relaxes bladder

* Also known as epinephrine and norepinephrine

When your sympathetic nervous system is activated, a series of physical changes occur that make sense if they are in response to a threat to your physical integrity. Some of these changes are listed below.

> Adrenaline is released so that you are alert and in a heightened state, ready to deal with the threat. This causes your heart rate to increase and can cause your hands, or even your whole body, to shake.

> Your hearing and your eyesight become better than normal. Everything sounds louder than it really is, and it is difficult to tolerate lots of light and movement. This is why anxious people tend to avoid places like supermarkets. Too much noise, too much light, and too much movement can be overwhelming when you feel anxious. Anxious people tend to tolerate these things poorly because of the acuteness of their senses when their sympathetic nervous systems are activated. It helps to have really good hearing and eyesight if you are being threatened, but it does not help if you are just trying to do some shopping.

In our view, the most amazing thing that happens is that your sympathetic nervous system shuts down the systems it does not need to be using. For example, when under threat, your body needs to produce lots of glucose for energy, so it stimulates glucose production. However, other systems that are not needed are shut down. In particular, your sympathetic nervous system shuts down your gastrointestinal system (e.g., inhibits digestion and inhibits peristalsis and secretion, with peristalsis referring to the contraction of the muscles that push forward the contents of your digestive tract). This is all right if it is shut down for the period of time it takes for you to deal with a truck coming around the corner. Your body copes less well with your gastrointestinal system not functioning if the sympathetic nervous system activation is prolonged. You can lose your appetite, experience nausea, develop diarrhoea or, less commonly, constipation, and you can experience difficulty eating, or you will overeat to try to control the uncomfortable state of your digestive system.

All of these reactions make sense if you are under threat but become a problem if the activation of your sympathetic nervous system is prolonged. Also, when your sympathetic nervous system is activated for reasons other than obvious threat, you can develop a sense of imminent danger just because your sympathetic nervous system has taken over your functioning. When your sympathetic nervous system is activated, your brain will interpret this as a sign that something is wrong. You will develop an overwhelming feeling that something terrible is about to happen, even in the absence of an identifiable sign of threat.

Later, we will introduce some straightforward ways you can bring your sympathetic nervous system under better control so your anxiety and fear are reduced. You can learn to control the messages being received because you are under pressure so that the message is not misinterpreted, and you can avoid the sense that something terrible is going to happen.

How will I cope?

The fact that you will have a strong and seemingly overwhelming emotional response to the breakdown of your relationship requires that you look for ways to cope. That is what we do when we are faced with problem situations in our lives... we try to use the skills we have to cope with our problems.

Coping

We all have our own coping resources and individual coping skills. Coping resources are the things we have available to use to help us cope, such as, family and friends. Coping skills are the strategies we are good at that we use to deal with the problems we face. We have our own particular coping resources and particular coping skills because there is no one particular way of coping.

In a general sense, the way you will cope with the relationship breakdown will likely be a reflection of the way you have dealt with and solved other problems throughout your life. That is, the way you cope will reflect your general style of coping.

Your goal should be to understand how you cope and to make good use of the coping resources you have or can create, as well as the particular skills you have developed or can develop. This is true even if you take into account the fact that the breakdown of the relationship may be a more challenging problem than other problems you have dealt with in your life. For those of you who feel you do not cope well with life problems, it may be the case you have been trying to develop coping skills based on a pattern of coping strategies that do not suit you.

To understand the way you cope and to use this knowledge to choose the best strategies to cope with the relationship breakdown, consideration needs to be given to the fundamental differences people can have in the way they approach problem situations. Let's consider the different approaches to coping so that you can work out your own preferred coping style.

Problem-focused coping vs. emotion-focused coping

To start, a distinction can be made between problem-focused coping strategies and emotion-focused strategies.

Who are problem-focused copers?

Problem-focused copers deal with their problems by considering the problem situation. They tend to want to *do* something when they are confronted with a problem. They are most comfortable when there are specific things related to the problem that can be the focus of their attention. In the context of a relationship disagreement, problem-focused copers are the people who will say, "Just tell me what I have to do to fix it", when when relationship issues are raised.

Who are emotion-focused copers?

Emotion-focused copers are the people who deal with their problems by expressing their emotional reactions to the situation. They will talk about the problem and cry when they feel the need. They see the value in looking to others to share their feelings about their problems. In the context of a relationship disagreement, the emotion-focused coper will say, "Just tell me how you are feeling" when dealing with their problem-focused partner and not understand when their partner seems incapable of or disinterested in doing so.

Are people either emotion-focused or problem-focused copers?

Some people are strongly problem-focused copers, and some people are strongly emotion-focused copers. Others fall somewhere on the continuum between the two extreme positions. You may be more problem-focused than emotion-focused, but still make use of some emotion-focused strategies… or the reverse.

You will be able to do a little exercise to find your coping preferences or to confirm them if you already have a good idea of where on the continuum you fall. But, first, we have to consider one other element.

Problem-approach vs. problem-avoidance coping

People assume that if we talk about coping strategies, they have to be good ones that will help us deal with the problems we face. This is not the case. People's coping style can be divided on the basis of whether they tend to front up to their problems or whether they prefer to avoid them. This is the case for both problem-focused copers and emotion-focused copers.

Let's start by looking at problem-focused coping. How would problem approach and problem avoidance strategies differ? Consider the examples in the table below.

Table 3: Examples of problem-focused approach and avoidance strategies.

Problem-focused, problem approach strategies	Problem-focused, problem avoidance strategies
Problem solving Problem solving coping strategies involve: • Examining the problem • Generating potential solutions • Evaluating the likelihood of a successful outcome • Moving forward and applying the strategy	*Problem avoidance* Problem avoidance coping strategies involve: • Deliberately avoiding thinking about the problem • Deliberately avoiding reminders of the problem
Cognitive restructuring Cognitive restructuring coping strategies involve: • Reframing your thoughts to think more reasonably about the problem • Correcting errors in thinking that are barriers to coping with the problem	*Wishful thinking* Wishful thinking as a coping strategy involves: • Wishing the problem would go away • Indulging in thoughts that things will return to 'normal' • Spending time thinking about how things will work out in your favour and as you wish

With regard to relationship breakdowns, the effective, problem-focused approach coping strategies may help in the following ways. They may help you think clearly about what needs to be done to resolve a problem situation. They can keep you focused on what you need to do without being overwhelmed by strong emotions. They can help you feel more in control.

Now, let's consider emotion-focused coping. The table below details examples of approach and avoidance emotion-focused coping strategies.

Table 4: Examples of emotion-focused approach and avoidance strategies.

Emotion-focused, problem approach strategies	Emotion-focused, problem avoidance strategies
Emotion expression Emotion expression as a coping strategy involves: • Being open and talking about how you are feeling • Allowing yourself to experience your emotional reactions in relation to the problem • Using emotion expression as a form of catharsis, letting off steam to allow yourself to feel better for a while	*Self-criticism* Self-criticism as a coping strategy involves: • Blaming yourself for the problem • Criticising yourself for failing to control your emotional reaction to the problem • Viewing yourself as more generally deficient than is warranted
Social support Using social support as a coping strategy involves: • Turning to family and friends for support • Talking with your support network about how you are feeling • Taking comfort from your support people • Allowing your support network to offer instrumental support*	*Social withdrawal* Social withdrawal as a coping strategy involves: • Cutting yourself off from family and friends • Failing to seek professional support when it is needed • Refusing assistance offered by the people who wish to help you or would be willing to do so

* Instrumental support refers to people undertaking helpful activities such as collection your children from school or cooking meals for you.

When we consider the breakup of your relationship, the effective emotion-focused approach coping strategies may be of assistance to you in the following ways. They can help you feel some relief when you feel overwhelmed by emotion. They can help you take advantage of your support network of family and friends. They can help you deal with the emotional roller coaster ride of emotions that you experience with this life crisis.

Identifying your preferred coping style

The goal here is to identify the type of coping that works best for you. If you are an emotion-focused coper, you may see the value of a problem-focused coping approach, but it is unlikely that you could comfortably adopt problem-focused coping strategies and expect them to work for you. Your efforts would be better directed at taking advantage of your preferred style of coping and using problem-approach strategies.

Here is an exercise in determining what type of coping style best characterises your preferred type. Tick the boxes if you typically use the listed coping strategies.

	How do I normally cope?
Problem solving	
	I work on finding ways to solve the problems I face.
	I work out what I should do, and then I follow the plan.
	I like to work out a plan and then move forward.
	I believe there is a solution to every problem.
Problem avoidance	
	I try to act like nothing is wrong.
	When faced with a problem, I choose not to do anything, even when I know I should.
	I try not to spend any time thinking about the problem.
	When the problem comes to mind, I push it out of my head.
Cognitive restructuring	
	I think about my problems in a way that allows me to realise I can manage them.
	I think about the problem to change the way I react to it.
	I try to look on the bright side of any situation.
	I try to put things into perspective.

Wishful thinking	
	When faced with a problem, I just wish it would go away.
	I just hope a miracle will happen to make everything all right.
	I hope the problem will fix itself.
	I wish that someone would come and fix the problem for me.
Emotion expression	
	When faced with a problem, I allow myself to express my feelings about it.
	I do not try to bottle up my feelings; I let them go so that I can feel better.
	I do not hide my feelings about the problem from other people.
	When faced with a problem, I just need some time to experience my feelings.
Self-criticism	
	I blame myself for the problem I am facing.
	I ask myself what I have done to make the problem happen.
	I tend to hold myself responsible for the problems I face.
	When a problem occurs, I feel I should have done things differently.
Social support	
	I turn to the people I know will listen when I talk about how I feel.
	I feel better when I can talk to others about my problems.
	When faced with a problem, I seek advice from people I trust.
	I allow other people to offer help and support when I am dealing with a problem.

Social withdrawal	
	When faced with a problem, I like to avoid other people and spend time by myself.
	When I am struggling with a problem, I do not want to be around other people.
	I do not share my thoughts and feelings with others.
	I do not accept the help others offer.

Checklist available at elemen.com.au

What type of coper are you? Add up the ticks you have placed in each of the categories and enter the number in the following table.

Ways of coping scoring sheet	
Problem-focused strategies	*Emotion-focused strategies*
_____ Problem-solving _____ Cognitive restructuring _____ Problem avoidance _____ Wishful thinking _____ **Total**	_____ Emotion expression _____ Social support _____ Self-criticism _____ Social withdrawal _____ **Total**
Problem-approach strategies	*Problem-avoidance strategies*
_____ Problem-solving _____ Cognitive restructuring _____ Emotion expression _____ Social support _____ **Total**	_____ Problem-avoidance _____ Wishful thinking _____ Self-criticism _____ Social withdrawal _____ **Total**

Score sheet available at elemen.com.au

When comparing your problem-focused and emotion-focused strategies, see where you have scored the highest. This may show a strong preference for one type of coping strategy or the other. If so, you can build on your preferred coping type when you consider what coping strategies will help you with your current situation. If you have similar totals for both problem-focused and emotion-focused strategies, you would do best to include each type in your coping plan.

When considering whether you use problem-approach strategies or problem-avoidance strategies, you are considering whether adjustments have to be made in the way you cope. If you predominantly use problem-avoidance strategies, you can learn to abandon those in favour of problem-approach strategies while staying within the same style of coping strategy, that is, problem-focused or emotion-focused.

We are going to come back to coping later in this workbook. There we will consider ways to build your coping strategies focusing on the types of strategies that will be most effective in helping you given your preferred coping style.

Why is my partner behaving like this?

It can seem quite confronting to be coping with the relationship breakdown in a way that appears so different to your previous partner's way of coping. There may be a number of reasons for this. Given what you now know about coping styles, it may be the case that your former partner copes in a different way to you. This difference in coping style may be reflected in the choices made of the way to cope with the breakdown of the relationship.

Further, it should also be remembered that, in all likelihood, the person ending the relationship has been thinking about doing so for some time. You are the person who has much more recently learned of this unfortunate and distressing experience. Even when the events that triggered the person to make the decision to leave the relationship occurred relatively recently, that person still has had greater time to think about this than have you. So, for you, it is relatively new information and you need to catch up.

In this way, your former partner may be coping with the situation differently because they are further along in the process of resolving the matter in their own mind. You should allow yourself the time you need to catch up and process this new information. Your former partner may be at a point where they feel they can make decisions about the future, but you may not be there yet. Do not feel pressured to make decisions before you are ready to do so.

What does my former partner's behaviour say about our lives together?

> *Rosemary tormented herself with thoughts about whether her relationship with her former partner was ever a loving one. She asked herself how her partner could ever have loved her if he was so insistent that he no longer cared for her and he hadn't been happy for a long time. She felt like she had been fooling herself into thinking that he had ever loved her. She felt stupid. She felt she should have known that the relationship was a fake.*

Despite the fact that your former partner is likely to cope differently than you and the fact that they may be in a different place in the process of resolving these relationship difficulties, it can be confronting to be treated as if your former partner no longer cares. This person is likely to have a history of considering your feelings and meeting your needs. Then, suddenly, this is no longer the case.

This tends to cause people in this position to question the meaning of their past relationship and whether the depth of feeling they assumed from their partner was ever the case. Often, this is not helped by comments that show that they have been unhappy for some time or that they have not loved you for a while. In a distressed state, you can easily jump to an incorrect conclusion that the loving basis of your relationship that you assumed had been the case was a sham.

It does not follow that the relationship was a sham. Nevertheless, it is apparent that the nature of the relationship has changed. At the beginning of a relationship both members of the relationship tend to be on the same pathway. You have enough in common to share your current interests and your wishes for the future. At the start of relationships, world views tend to be similar. However, over time, this can change.

It is not unreasonable to suppose that people's perspectives alter. We understand that we change and grow during childhood and adolescence. However, people tend not to realise that we continue to change and develop throughout our adult lives as well. It makes more sense if you consider the differences between what we might want in our twenties and what we might want in our fifties. In many ways, it is quite a challenge for people to remain on matching pathways throughout their adult lives. It may be factors such as shared values that hold couples together.

Even as these pathways diverge and feelings start to change, we often try to pretend that things remain the same. It is difficult to give up something that is familiar and stable for an uncertain future. Then, a realisation occurs, for whatever reason, that life is not satisfactory. Looking back, they realise that this dissatisfaction has been present for some time, and the dissatisfaction is labelled as unhappiness. In ending the relationship, one party will often say they have not been happy for a long time. This can be more a case of reflection and reinterpretation than actually representing a life of misery. The way this information is conveyed to you can be hurtful, but it is not an indication that the whole of your relationship was other than what you thought.

But why are they being so unfeeling?

> *Carl was shocked by his former partner's behaviour towards him. She knew how upset he was about her leaving, but she just didn't seem to care. He thought she would understand how hard it was for him and comfort him or give him some support or something other than the coldness he was receiving from her. He tried calling her one evening just because he felt so distressed and needed to talk to her, but she was really short with him. When he tried to call on another occasion, she didn't answer, and she didn't return his call when he left her a message.*

After a relationship ends, even in the immediate aftermath of that experience, a partner who used to be concerned about your well-being can suddenly present as if they do not care that you are suffering. It can seem like the person you were certain you knew well is now acting like a stranger.

Although nothing should excuse hurtful behaviour, it may help you if you can understand the psychological processes behind this change. This is not to excuse the hurtful behaviour. It has more to do with your understanding that there are events occurring that are not related to you or your worthiness.

At the end of a relationship there occurs a period of disengagement. This is where a person is trying to separate themselves emotionally from another person. Many people struggle to do this in a way that is reasonable and gentle, taking into account the needs of the other person.

So, what does this process of disengaging mean? We are referring to a process of emotionally distancing yourself from another person with whom you used to have a close relationship. This is done in an effort to adjust to the change in life circumstances. To better understand this process, it is worth considering the nature and strength of the bonds people form with each other.

The influence of attachment

The closeness of a relationship reflects the bond that has developed between two people. An attachment forms between two people and this attachment ensures the connection between those people.

You have probably heard of attachment as it relates to a parent and child. An attachment relationship develops between the child and the parent so that the child receives the attention he or she needs. For a child to develop normally, that relationship should be characterised by warmth, empathic involvement and continuity over time.

Adults also form attachments with the significant people in their lives. Loving feelings reflect the bond that has developed between the two people. This bond exists because of the same three features that need to be present in attachment relationships between a parent and child. That is, a close, loving bond is characterised by warmth between the two people, closeness or empathic involvement, and continuity of contact. For a bond to be strong, all three features need to be present. If one or more of those features change, the strength of the relationship tends to change.

The function of these features can also be used by a person who deliberately chooses to break away from a relationship. Although it can be argued that one or more of the features would already have had to have changed for the desire to break away to be present, it may be the case that to entirely extinguish a sense of attachment, a person may choose to withdraw any residual warm feelings, abandon the sense of empathic involvement or closeness, and break off the continuity of contact.

It should also be noted that the partner who decides to leave and has been thinking about doing so for some time has already become involved in a process of disengagement from the attachment relationship. The other person in the partnership may still feel a stronger attachment bond than the person who has already decided to disengage and leave.

It is worth noting that the process of disengagement and the reduction in the strength of the attachment relationship may explain your former partner's colder behaviour. While you still retain a stronger sense of attachment, even if it has been damaged by relationship changes, your former partner, who has had more opportunities to go through the process of disengagement, does not.

It may help to keep this information in mind when you are hurt by it and trying to understand the change in behaviour and attitude demonstrated by your former partner. Although your former partner might not be handling the process well or in a way that spares your feelings, in effect, it is a normal process. Not only that, but it is a process that you will experience as well after you have begun disengaging. You will find that your feelings for the other person are not as strong. Although it is hard to imagine at this point, it too will be a natural process that you will experience. It is a process that you do not have to fight or change, either in terms of hanging on or letting go. It is a natural consequence of changes to those three features of warmth, empathic involvement and continuity of contact.

What can I do to feel better?

While you are waiting for a natural process of disengagement to occur, there are a variety of strategies you can use to help you deal with your reaction to the breakdown of your relationship. These are aimed at helping you cope with your distress, and to feel more in control.

> You can learn to have some control over what your sympathetic nervous system is doing. This part of your nervous system controls your sense of anxious arousal. Your sympathetic nervous system may be reacting to the crisis you are experiencing as if the crisis were physically threatening you. By learning how to control what is happening with your sympathetic nervous system, the feeling of threat should be reduced.
>
> You can learn to manage sleep problems when a good night's sleep seems unattainable.
>
> By learning some techniques to help you regulate your emotions, you can exert some control over the intensity of the emotional reactions you feel. This is important during the emotional roller coaster ride stage of your reaction to this crisis in your life you are experiencing.
>
> To further your ability to regulate your emotions, you can learn some anger management skills. Anger is a normal part of people's reaction to relationship breakdowns. Learning to control your anger will help you feel like you have better control of your emotional state.
>
> You can learn acceptance of what has happened. This protects you from the torment of 'what ifs…' and 'if only….' that can overwhelm your thoughts and cause you to feel distressed.
>
> By understanding that the way you think about an experience strongly influences your emotional reaction to that event, you can learn some strategies that will allow you to think about what is happening in ways that make the relationship breakdown seem more manageable.
>
> You can build on your existing coping strategies and learn new ways of coping with the relationship breakdown that will allow you to react to stressful events in ways that reduce distress. By understanding your preferred coping style, you can ensure that the coping strategies you choose are ones that are easier for you to adopt and are more effective for you.

You can learn to look after yourself at a time when self-care is so important.

Let's learn some techniques that may help you. As these techniques are introduced, consider them and try them out. Choose the ones that you feel will help you the most.

Controlling your sympathetic nervous system

As described earlier, it is likely that your sympathetic nervous system has been responding to this crisis in your life as if it were a threat to your physical integrity. When this occurs, you experience a number of physical changes that place your system into a self-protective state. You need strategies that will send a message to your nervous system that you are safe.

Range of arousal

Before considering ways to achieve this, we need to look at one other feature of your nervous system. It is worth noting that human beings have a range of nervous system arousal within which we function the best. This range is quite large, from low in the range when we are very relaxed to high in the range when our nervous system is most 'revved up'. Pictured below is a diagram of this arousal range. The range within which you function best is known as the *window of tolerance*.

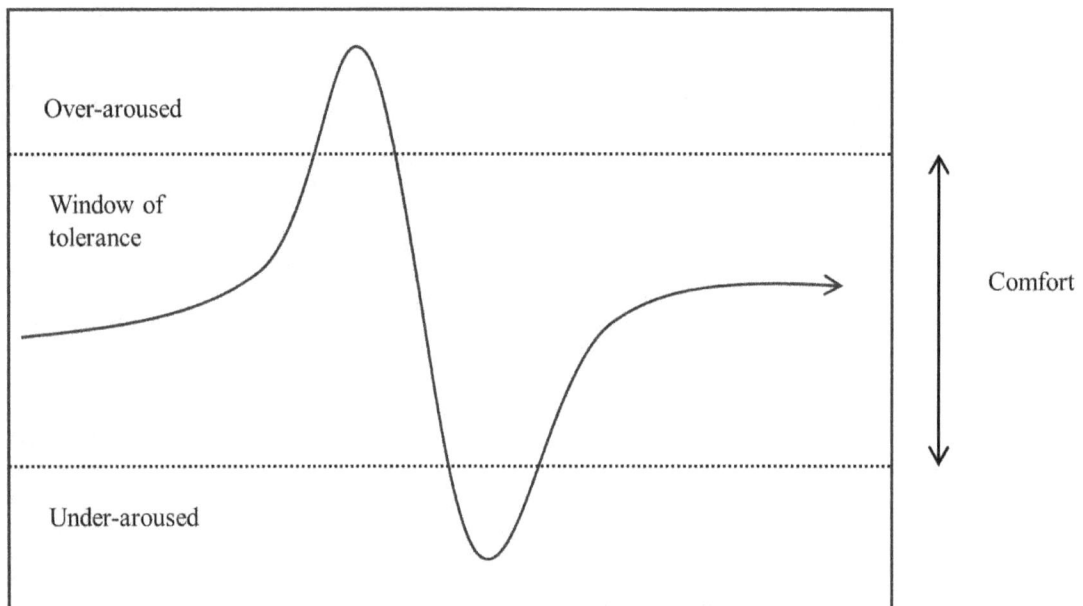

Figure 1: A diagram of the window of tolerance.

Within this window of tolerance, you have the flexibility to respond to the demands being placed on you. In this way, your arousal level will increase when you are faced with a demand and then decrease when that demand is over. As long as your arousal stays within this window, you will respond well to pressures placed on you.

If your arousal level drops below the lowest point of that range, you will enter a state of hypoarousal. In this state, you will feel slowed down and lethargic. Your functioning at this point will be inadequate, and your ability to respond to demands will be poor. If your arousal increases beyond the ceiling level, you will enter a state of hyperarousal. When this occurs, you can feel too aroused and can feel anxious and panicky. Your functioning will be impacted, and your ability to cope with pressures will deteriorate.

When you have been too stressed for a while or when you are faced with significant challenges but are still managing to cope, your arousal level creeps up from an optimal level of arousal in the middle of the window of tolerance to the upper extremes. You will find that you cannot or do not reduce that high level of arousal, even when you should be able to let go. This is why people cannot sleep well when they are under pressure. They can never relax enough for their arousal to decrease to a comfortable state. So, your 'baseline' arousal level, which is the starting point from which you respond to life demands, is high up in the range instead of midway or lower in the window of tolerance.

In this case, your arousal level remains elevated. You barely notice this because it starts to feel normal to be under that much stress with your arousal level that high. But a problem exists. When any other thing occurs to which you have to respond, your arousal level will increase to deal with that additional demand being placed on you. However, when the starting point of your arousal level, or your baseline arousal level, is already so high, you have no room to move. Any increase in arousal will push you through the ceiling and into an uncomfortable and unpleasant hyperaroused state. You will experience anxiety as a result.

Your high starting point gives you no flexibility to respond or react to even minor additional stressors. So, the ways you normally cope with demanding situations fail because you have moved out of the range where you can successfully apply your usual coping strategies.

Anxiety management strategies

Your goal should be to get your nervous system back under control. Dealing with the challenges you face or worrying too much about the future has likely pushed your arousal level to the upper limits of your window of tolerance. Extra demands, even minor ones, then cause your arousal level to move beyond the ceiling of the window of tolerance and uncomfortable and unpleasant anxiety symptoms are then experienced.

You need to aim to bring your optimal arousal level down to at least the middle of the window of tolerance, with a baseline or starting point, when you are at your most relaxed, to the lower end of that range. You need to teach your nervous system to have a better starting point and a better optimal arousal level.

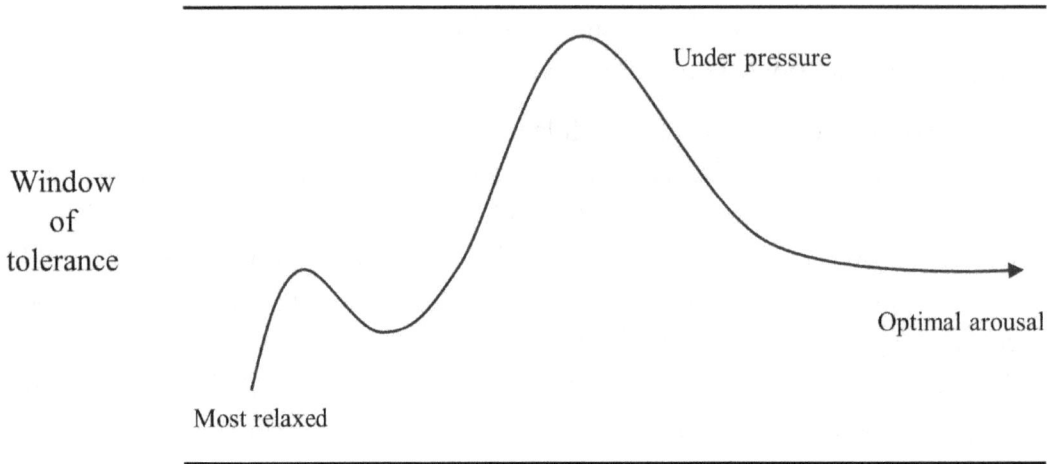

Figure 2: A diagram of an optimal level of arousal.

Breathing and heart rate

How do you achieve this? Consider the following. When you are in an elevated or heightened state, at the top of your window of tolerance or beyond it, your heart rate increases and your breathing changes. Your heart rate elevation is caused by a release of adrenaline that occurs when your sympathetic nervous system is triggered. This can be very uncomfortable, and it feels like there is very little you can do about it.

Your breathing changes contribute to the elevation in your heart rate. When people are stressed, their breathing tends to be rapid and shallow. You can liken this pattern of breathing to the waves on top of the water. Form a picture in your mind of the way a child draws waves. When we are stressed, we tend to breathe in sharply, then breathe out quickly and then breathe in again quickly. We tend not to breathe all the way out before we breathe in again. This inhalation-exhalation pattern is what affects your heart rate.

In contrast, when we are relaxed, our breathing tends to be deeper and slower and has a pattern than is similar to the swell in the ocean. The inhalation-exhalation pattern is a comfortable breath-in followed by a long, slower breath-out. We do not breathe in again until we have breathed all the way out.

From the diagram below, you can see the pattern of anxious, rapid and shallow breathing on the top. Below that is the pattern of slower, deeper breathing that is characteristic of a more relaxed state.

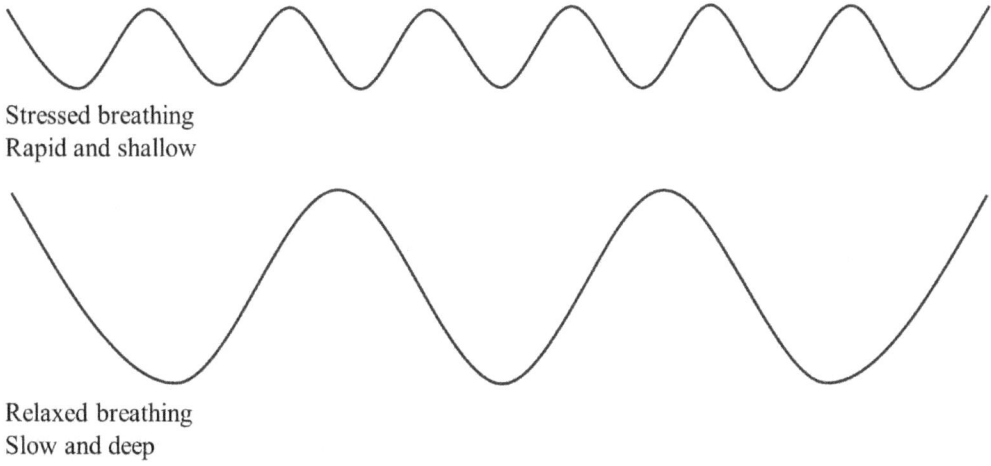

Figure 3: A comparison between stressed and relaxed breathing.

The reason your breathing pattern affects your heart rate is because these two things are linked. Under normal, stress-free conditions, you heart rate increases as you breathe in and then slows as you breathe out. This is normal. When you are stressed and your respiration rate increases and your breathing is shallower, your heart rate does not have a chance to slow before you breathe in again. Therefore, your heart rate is elevated and stays up.

Let's, for a moment, go back to the truck speeding around the corner, threatening to run you over. Your sympathetic nervous system is activated, allowing you to be in the right physical state to move quickly out of harm's way and protect yourself. When you get to the other side of the road, the truck goes past and you are unharmed, your brain registers these experiences and your sympathetic nervous system turns off and your parasympathetic nervous system takes over. This is because reaching the other side of the road and seeing the truck pass you by are safety signals. Your brain interprets these signs as indicators that you are going to be all right.

Of course, no such safety signals are available when your relationship has broken down, when you are sitting in your loungeroom worrying, or when you are shopping at the supermarket. They are not that sort of event. Your brain would struggle to identify safety indicators because they do not exist in that sort of form. What you can do is offer your brain a safety signal but of a different type.

Breathing and muscle tension exercises

You can send a message that everything is all right by deliberately slowing your heart rate from its elevated rate to a more normal rate for you. Although it sounds difficult to achieve, that is controlling your heart rate, it actually is a reasonably straightforward undertaking. If you slow your breathing and lengthen your exhalation until you have breathed all the way out before breathing back in, your heart rate will come into line, and your heart rate will go down.

To use our waves and ocean swell analogy, the aim is to change the pattern of your breathing from waves on the top of the water to a pattern like the swell in the ocean, where the water is lifted up and then put back down as the swell passes. You are aiming for an easy, comfortable breath in, followed by a long, slow breath out.

The ideal situation is to breathe out for twice as long as it takes you to breathe in. Elongating your exhalation requires that you slow the amount of air you breathe out so that you can breathe out for longer. You should aim to breathe all the way out, emptying your lungs, before you gently and comfortably breathe back in.

This pattern of breathing should result in a slowed heart rate and a subsequent reduction in that sense of anxiety or crisis that occurs when your sympathetic nervous system is triggered. This occurs because your brain interprets the reduction in heart rate and the change in breathing pattern as a signal that the crisis is over.

Let's consider a simple exercise to control your breathing by deepening your breaths and slowing them down.

	Slowing and controlling your breathing
1.	Without trying to change your breathing, just notice for a moment the pattern of your inhalations and exhalations.
2.	Now, take a comfortable breath in. It does not have to be too deep, rather just a comfortable breath.
3.	Now, breathe out, slowing the amount of air you exhale and lengthening your breath as a result.
4.	When your lungs feel empty of air, gently and comfortably breathe back in.
5.	As you breathe, practice lengthening your exhalation just a bit. You may also deepen your breath in slightly. Keep in mind the picture of the ocean swell if this helps.
6.	Practice this pattern of breathing for as long as you feel comfortable.

Exercise available at elemen.com.au

There is another element that you can add to this breathing exercise that may help with your ultimate goal of reducing your anxiety and signalling your sympathetic nervous system to turn off so your parasympathetic nervous system can do its job. You can include in this breathing exercise the element of reducing your muscle tension.

People who are stressed tend to have tense muscles. Although this muscle tension can occur anywhere in the body, common sites include the forehead and scalp, neck, jaw, shoulders, and chest. The increased muscle tension contributes to the overall sense of readiness to deal with threat. On the downside, tense muscles can cause headaches, chest and other pain.

If tense muscles present a significant problem for you, then a progressive muscle relaxation exercise may help. A general overview of this technique is provided below. More comprehensive versions are available online. However, another easy strategy is to link the relaxation of muscles with the breathing exercise.

As you breathe out, just relax your muscles in places where they feel tight and tense. You do not have to achieve marked muscle relaxation to experience a noticeable difference. Just drop your shoulders, relax your jaw, smooth your forehead or relax your stomach muscles. Aim for a gentle relaxation of tight muscles as you exhale.

The combination of breathing exercise and muscle relaxation can be used even when the focus is on controlling your breathing. You can also use the combined technique when your primary focus is on troubling muscle tension. In combination, the techniques can help with either target.

	Combined breathing and muscle relaxation technique
1.	Take a comfortable breath in. It does not have to be too deep, rather just a comfortable breath.
2.	Now, breathe out, slowing the amount of air you exhale and lengthening your breath as a result. As you breathe out, drop your shoulders, relax your jaw, smooth your forehead and relax your abdominal muscles.
3.	When your lungs feel empty of air, gently and comfortably breathe back in.
4.	As you breathe, practice lengthening your exhalation just a bit. You may also deepen your breath in slightly. Keep in mind the picture of the ocean swell if this helps. Continue to relax your muscles slightly on each exhalation.
5.	Practice this pattern of breathing and muscle relaxation for as long as you feel comfortable.

Exercise available at elemen.com.au

As stated, if muscle tension presents you with a significant problem, you may wish to try a method of progressive muscle relaxation. This technique involves tensing your muscles and then relaxing them. Tensing your muscles before relaxing them has a number of purposes. It helps you to clearly identify where the tension in your body is located. It helps you feel the difference between a tense muscle and a relaxed one, which is helpful when the muscle has been tense for a long time. Finally, tensing the muscle first helps to induce deeper relaxation in that muscle when you relax it.

We will start with a longer version of the progressive muscle relaxation exercise that will help you learn the technique. You can then change to a shorter version that we describe below.

	Progressive muscle relaxation (longer version)
1.	Choose a comfortable place where it is quiet. Lay down or sit in a comfortable position with your feet flat on the floor.
2.	Now clench both your fists… tighter and tighter. Notice the tension in your muscles. Keep it clenched for about 10 seconds. Now relax. Feel your muscles relax. Notice the difference between the tension and relaxation.
3.	Repeat the procedure again with your fists. Notice the difference between tension and relaxation.
4.	Now bend your elbows on both arms and tense your biceps. Hold the tension. Now relax. Notice the difference between tension and relaxation.
5.	Repeat the procedure again with your elbows bent and your biceps tensed. Hold the tension, then relax. Pay attention to the change from tension to relaxation.
6.	Now, frown as hard as you can. Notice the tension in your forehead. Hold the tension. Now relax. Notice the difference you feel after you have released the tension.
7.	Now frown again as hard as you can. Hold the tension, then release it. Notice the contrast between tension and relaxation.
8.	Now close your eyes and squint them tightly. Hold the tension then relax. Allow your eyes to feel a comfortable relaxed state. Notice the change. Repeat by closing your eyes and squinting then relaxing, letting go of the tension.
9.	Now, clench your jaw. Bite down hard. Notice the tension throughout your jaw. Now, relax your jaw, allowing your teeth to fall apart slightly. Notice the feeling of relaxation. Repeat this exercise with your jaw.
10.	Now press your tongue hard against the roof of your mouth. Hold it there. Feel the tension at the back of your mouth. Now relax. Notice the difference between the tension and relaxation. Repeat the exercise with your tongue.

11.	Now, purse your lips, pushing them out into an 'O' shape. Hold them there. Now release the tension and relax. Notice how your mouth feels now that it is relaxed. Repeat the exercise with your lips.
12.	Now press your head back as far as it will comfortably go. Hold onto the tension. Roll your head from the right to the left, allowing the focus of the tension to change. Now relax. Feel the difference between the tension in your neck and the relaxation. Repeat the exercise by pressing your head back.
13.	Now, bring your head forward with your chin on your chest. Feel the tension in your throat and the back of your neck. Hold the tension, then relax and allow your head to return to a comfortable position. Repeat the exercise by bringing your head forward.
14.	Now, shrug your shoulders, bringing your shoulders up and allowing your head to hunch down between them. Hold the tension. Now relax and notice the difference between tension and relaxation.
15.	Now, breathe in deeply and hold your breathe. Hold it. Now allow yourself to gently exhale, letting go of tension as you breathe out. Feel your body relax. Repeat the exercise, breathing in then gently letting go.
16.	Now, tense your stomach muscles. Hold onto the tension. Now relax. Let your stomach muscles relax and appreciate that feeling. Repeat the exercise with your stomach muscles.
17.	Now, arch your back without straining. Hold onto the tension. Now let it go. Notice the change in your muscles. Now repeat the exercise by arching your back.
18.	Now tighten your buttocks and thighs. Press down on your heels to flex your thigh muscles. Hold onto the tension. Now relax and notice the difference. Repeat the exercise.
19.	Now curl your toes downward to cause your calves to tense. Hold onto the tension. Now relax. Repeat the exercise.
20.	Now, draw your toes upward, causing your shins to feel tense. Pay attention to the tension. Now relax. Repeat the exercise.

21.	Now, scan your body. Notice if there are any tense spots. Repeat the exercise in that area.
22.	Enjoy the more relaxed feeling throughout your entire body. When you are ready, slowly return to your normal activities, holding on to that feeling of relaxation.

Exercise available at elemen.com.au

Once you have learned the technique, you can use a shorter version. You may prefer to just focus on the areas of your body that are particularly tense. It is certainly the case that some people tend to carry their muscle tension in one or two areas. Here is a shorter version that will allow you to tailor the procedure to suit your own needs.

Relaxing using progressive muscle relaxation (short version)	
1.	Choose a comfortable place where it is quiet. Lay down or sit in a comfortable position with your feet flat on the floor.
2.	Begin to work your way through groups of muscles by tensing them and relaxing them. For example, if you start with your forehead, tighten the muscles in your forehead by frowning. Hold for a few moments (10-15 seconds), then release, allowing the muscle in your forehead to relax, enjoying that experience for about 60 seconds. Notice the difference between the tension and the relaxation.
3.	Then, move on to the next group of muscles. You can work through groups of muscles from the top of your head to the tips of your toes, or you can select areas of your body that present a particular problem of tension for you.
4.	Repeat the process until you have worked your way through the groups of muscles you have selected.
5.	Repeat that process again, first tensing the muscles, holding that tension for five to ten seconds, and then relaxing those muscles.

Exercise available at elemen.com.au

So, controlling your breathing and, thus, lowering your heart rate will help you feel less anxious, as will reducing your muscle tension. However, there are other approaches you can take to manage your anxiety.

Quieting your mind

One of the problems with being anxious and 'revved up' is that your mind fills up with anxiety-provoking thoughts. When you are dealing with a demanding situation and have too many things to worry about, you cannot seem to stop thinking in an endless stream of anxiety-provoking thoughts. This makes it very difficult to get your nervous system back under control. The thoughts racing through your mind do not allow you to relax. So, included here are some exercises that may help you settle your mind.

The first exercises aim to teach you to self-soothe. If you can learn to settle yourself, the racing thoughts in your mind may follow. The quieter your nervous system, the less active your mind is with anxiety-provoking thoughts.

What you are aiming to do is find ways to soothe yourself. Most of us can understand how we go about soothing an upset child. We might hold and rock a distressed child and say soothing things. What you are looking for are adult versions of self-soothing strategies that will help to alleviate your distressed state.

The goal of developing self-soothing strategies is to create for yourself some moments of less distress. The strategies are aimed at reducing your heightened state to a more manageable level. They allow your nervous system arousal level to be brought back under your control. So, strategies that allow you to focus on the here and now are the ones that will allow you to choose to be in a quieter state with a greater sense of peace of mind.

Consider the proposed self-soothing strategies listed below and select ones that you think might assist you. These may be things you have tried before or ones you feel might work for you. Some of these strategies require you to make the effort to seek out the means of engaging with them. However, others are using things that are readily available or easily obtained.

	Self-soothing strategies
	Take a shower or a warm bath. Focus your attention on the sensations created by the water. Enjoy the feeling of the water on your skin and the warmth of the water.
	Play with your pet, or just stroke your dog's or cat's coat. Interacting with your pet has been demonstrated to be soothing for many pet owners.
	Change into your most comfortable clothes. Enjoy the feel of the fabric and the degree of comfort you feel from wearing these items of clothing.
	Go for a swim. Enjoy the sensation of being in the water. Allow those sensations to quiet your mind. Even if you are not a good swimmer, bobbing around in the water can produce the same sensations.

	Treat yourself to a massage if that appeals to you. Allow your muscles to relax and your mind to quiet.
	Listen to soothing music. Allow your attention to be directed to the music rather than have the music in the background.
	Listen to an audiobook, even if your distress makes it difficult to concentrate. Try to pay attention to each word that is spoken. If you lose track of the story, you can always return to the previous track and pick up the story again.
	Turn on the television or talkback radio and engage in listening to what is being broadcast. The goal here is to focus your attention on the conversations as they play out rather than selecting a programme you are excited to watch or listen to. It is the process of listening to others talking that is soothing.
	Listen to the sounds of water running. Again, the aim is to listen to the sounds of the water, stopping your mind from going to other intrusive thoughts. You can find the sound of running water in various places. You can visit a naturally occurring water course or waterfall. You could listen to running water from an outdoor garden fountain. However, you can also get an indoor personal fountain that can be used at any time. Alternatively, you can listen to recorded sounds of water running.
	Find something soothing to look at. This might be by the water or an outdoor space such as a park. It could be photographs or paintings that you find soothing or relaxing. The goal is to find something to look at that is engaging for you, and that you find relaxing and soothing.
	Spend some time outside in nature. Notice the freshness of the air. See the colours around you. Feel the breeze on your face. Notice the smell of the plants. Listen to the natural sounds around you.

Exercise available at elemen.com.au

Building on this notion of self-soothing, it is a good idea to be more present in your focus. If you give it some consideration, you will find that the thoughts racing through your mind when you are anxious typically are not related to what is happening here and now. Our thoughts tend to engage in time-travelling, that is, they are focused either on what has already happened or what is to come. They rarely focus on what is happening in the present moment when you are trying to relax.

Usually, in the present moment, nothing is happening that is worth worrying about. If you could deliberately spend more time focused on the here and now and less time on the past or future, you would have a better chance of relaxing and quieting your overly stimulated nervous system.

The notion of focusing on the here and now is based on mindfulness techniques. Mindfulness refers to your ability to be aware of your emotions, your physical state, your actions and your thoughts in a state of mind that is absent from judgment or criticism of your experience. Research has demonstrated that mindfulness helps you to control symptoms of anxiety, to control the distress caused by particular situations, to increase your capacity to relax, and to learn how to cope better with challenging situations.

Based on the notion of mindfulness, we have included some exercises you can use to quiet your mind by focusing on the here and now. To do this well, you may need to practice the skill. When you first learn these techniques, it is easy to become distracted and return to your racing thoughts. Do not worry if this happens. Just return to your exercise and continue.

	Mindful listening
1.	Sit in a comfortable place, preferably by yourself. If you wish, close your eyes.
2.	Start to focus your attention on the sounds around you.
3.	Notice the changes in the sounds from moment to moment.
4.	Notice the times between sounds when it is quiet.
5.	Focus your attention both on what is happening inside and outside.
6.	Pay attention to the sounds and nothing else. Do not make judgments about the sounds. Just acknowledge the sound then listen to the next one.
7.	If thoughts about other things come into your mind, put them to one side then return to listening to the sounds around you.
8.	Do this for a few minutes or until you are ready to stop.

Exercise available at elemen.com.au

Let's try another mindfulness exercise.

	Mindful use of your senses
Sight	Look around you. Allow your attention to be drawn to five things in your immediate environment that you might not normally pay any attention to. For example, this might be the way the fruit is sitting in the fruit bowl, the way your curtain is hanging, or the way your books are placed on your bookcase. Allow your attention to rest on each of these things. Keep your focus directed at the item, setting aside any other thoughts that come into your mind.
Touch	Bring your attention to four things you can feel at this moment in time. For example, it may be the feel of the sun on your skin, or the feel of the fabric of your clothes against your skin, or the feel of the chair underneath you, or the feel of the table surface where your hand is resting. Allow your attention to rest on each of these feelings. Keep your focus directed at each sense of touch, setting aside any other thoughts that come into your mind.
Hearing	Listen to the sounds in your surroundings. Notice three things you can hear. For example, you might hear the sounds of cars travelling along the road, or the noise of the refrigerator, or the sound of the wind in the trees. Focus your attention on each of these sounds. If other thoughts come into your mind, let those thoughts go and return to focusing on the sounds you can hear.
Smell	Pay attention and search for two things you can smell. For example, you might be able to smell whatever you are cooking, the scent of plants in your garden, or the sea air if you live near the water. Keep your attention focused on each of these smells. If other distracting thoughts come into your mind, let these thoughts go and return to focusing on the things you can smell.
Taste	When you are eating, focus your attention on the tastes you are experiencing. For example, take a sip of your coffee and notice the taste. Bite into your sandwich and notice the flavours. Really pay attention to the flavours of the things you are tasting. If you become distracted, let go of these interfering thoughts and return to focusing on the things you are tasting.

Exercise available at elemen.com.au

And there is one last mindfulness exercise.

	Mindful walking
1.	As you are ready for your walk, stand still for a moment. Sense the weight on your feet as your stand there. Feel how your muscles are supporting you and maintaining your stability and balance. Be aware of your arms in a comfortable position of your choice (e.g., by your side or hands clasped, either at the front or at your back). Allow yourself to stand there, relaxed but alert.
2.	Begin to walk. Choose a comfortable pace, not too fast and not too slow. Pay attention to how your feet and legs feel (e.g., their heaviness or lightness, the energy, or even any pain). The way your legs and feet feel will form the focus of your attention. If you become distracted, return to focusing on your legs and feet.
3.	Pay attention to the way in which you lift your feet and place them back down on the surface on which you are walking. Notice how you lift your foot, swing your leg and place your foot down again ahead of where you were a moment before. Walk in a natural and relaxed manner. Move your arms in a way that feels normal for you.
4.	It is likely that your mind will wander as you walk along. Your attention will be drawn to what is around you or thoughts that come into your mind. Acknowledge that you have been distracted and return to focusing on the process of walking… the lifting of your foot, the swing of your leg and the placement of your foot in front of you. Just gently return your attention to the sensations of walking.
5.	You might focus on a point ahead of you. Focus on the steps you take as you move towards that point. One step at a time. Experience fully the sensations of walking.
6.	Keep walking mindfully until you reach your destination or the point where you decide to turn around and mindfully walk back to where you started.

Exercise available at elemen.com.au

These types of strategies can help deal with another manifestation of too much stress and too much anxiety, that is, sleep disturbance. Let's consider this next.

Dealing with sleep disturbance

One of the consequences of your nervous system being revved up and having too many stressful thoughts is that your sleep can become disturbed. You can become fatigued as a consequence and it becomes more difficult for you to cope with the demands of your day.

There are three types of insomnia. You might experience any one or all three of these types of sleep problems.

1. *Trouble going to sleep.* This is where you are unable to go to sleep despite being tired.
2. *Trouble staying asleep.* This is where you repeatedly wake throughout the night, but after a period of time, you are able to go back to sleep.
3. *Waking early and being unable to go back to sleep.* This is where you wake early in the morning, and despite needing more sleep, you cannot return to sleep.

Each of these types of sleep problems is understandable if you take into consideration your stages of sleep.

Table 5: A description of the stages of sleep.

Stages of sleep	
Stage 1	This is a transitional stage from wakefulness to sleep. It is associated with very light sleep. During this stage, muscle activity slows down.
Stage 2	During this stage, your sleep starts to deepen. Your breathing pattern changes and slows as does your heart rate. Your body temperature drops slightly.
Stage 3	It is at this stage that deep sleep begins to be experienced. To signal the onset of deep sleep, your brain starts to generate slow delta waves.
Stage 4	This is when you are most deeply asleep. During this stage, your muscle activity is limited.
REM sleep	This refers to Rapid Eye Movement Sleep. It occurs when you are at the closest point to wakefulness. It is associated with vivid dreaming. During this stage, your heart rate increases.

Over the course of the night, you will cycle through these stages. For the first half or so of the night, you will cycle down into the deep sleep associated with stages 3 and 4. However, as the night progresses, the cycling pattern is lighter and does not involve deep sleep. This pattern is demonstrated in the diagram below. Periods of REM sleep occur at the point in the cycle when you are closest to waking.

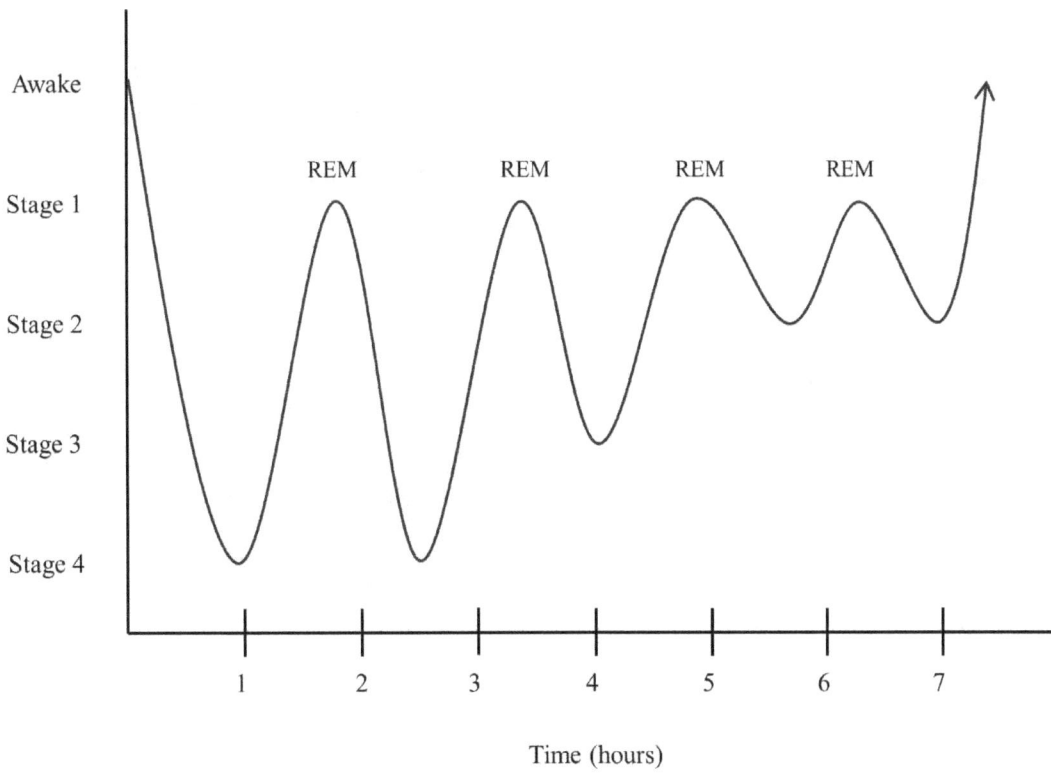

Figure 4: The cycles of sleep over the course of a sleep period.

When you have trouble falling asleep at the beginning of the night, you are struggling to enter into Stage 1 of sleep. This transitional stage is designed to pull you down into deeper sleep. Stage 1 allows you to do what your brain is inviting you to do, that is, go to sleep. Unfortunately, if you are stressed, your nervous system is generally too aroused to allow this to occur. Your nervous system fights against this natural urge to sleep. Your stressful thoughts are indicating to your brain that it is a good idea to stay awake in case something happens to which you need to respond.

When you have trouble staying asleep, you tend to wake up when your sleep cycle reaches those points where it is closest to wakefulness. In general, your nervous system is too aroused to allow you to stay asleep. Then, as soon as you wake, your mind turns to stressful thoughts that then keep you awake until you can get back to sleep. This can happen many times throughout the night.

When you are troubled by waking early and being unable to return to sleep, this usually occurs in the second part of the night when you have moved past the deep sleep cycles. Your sleep is lighter, and when your nervous system is too aroused, and you come close to wakefulness, you become completely awake, your stressful thoughts begin, and you cannot get back to sleep.

What can I do about my sleep problems?

Each of these types of sleep disturbance can be influenced by racing thoughts. These thoughts are usually of a stressful nature. They increase your nervous system arousal, making it difficult to get any rest. You are especially likely to be bothered by such thoughts at night because there is nothing else going on to distract you from these thoughts.

Here is a series of simple steps that should help you have a better night's sleep.

	Simple sleep strategy
1.	In the evening, avoid caffeine and sugary drinks and food.
2.	In the lead-up to your bedtime, start to wind down. Turn off stimulating television or stop engaging in other activities around the house that cause you to feel more alert.
3.	Have a small snack rich in carbohydrates.
4.	Get into a comfortable bed and into a comfortable position. Slow your breathing. Relax your muscle tension.
5.	Give your mind something to think about that is not emotionally arousing. This could be writing a simple story in your head, listing in your mind all the countries you can think of, starting with A, then B, etc. Count backwards by 7s from a randomly selected number.
6.	If your mind drifts to more stressful thoughts, acknowledge that is what is happening then return to the activity you chose to keep your mind focused.
7.	Allow yourself to drift off to sleep.

Exercise available at elemen.com.au

The goal here is to create the right sort of internal environment to facilitate a good night's sleep. Avoid caffeine and sugary food or drinks because they can have a stimulating effect on your nervous system. In general, you should be aiming to 'turn off' by reducing the number of external stimulating activities. You do these things in preparation for sleep.

Carbohydrates can also increase your readiness for sleep. This is because carbohydrates contribute to an increase in your brain of a protein called tryptophan. This is a building block for a neurotransmitter called serotonin and a hormone called melatonin. Serotonin has a role in controlling sleep, appetite and mood. Melatonin release is triggered by darkness, and this hormone helps promote a regular sleep-wake cycle. This process, triggered by eating a carbohydrate-rich snack before bedtime, helps you sleep.

When your mind is already overrun by thoughts that are keeping you awake, it seems counterintuitive to give your brain something else to think about. However, it is not the thoughts themselves that will keep you awake. It is the nature of the thoughts that will have an effect on your sleep. In this way, you want to distract yourself from thinking stress-related thoughts, replacing them with thoughts that will not cause you to react emotionally. You should aim to keep your brain busy with mundane thoughts so that your mind is distracted from the stress-inducing thoughts. We like to refer to this activity as 'busy work' for your brain. It is the modern-day equivalent of counting sheep.

Mundane thoughts will allow you to drift off to sleep, whereas stress-related thoughts will keep you alert and awake. Your brain is always active, so it is not possible for you to stop thinking. When you think of things that cause your nervous system to respond by increasing your arousal, you will have trouble sleeping. If you think calming or even boring thoughts, your brain will trigger the processes that lead you to falling asleep.

The same strategy of giving your mind something other than stressful things to think about can be applied if you awaken during the night. Simply get settled and focus on the mundane thoughts you have selected, allowing yourself to drift off back to sleep.

Regulating your emotions

As we have described, experiencing a life crisis, such as the breakdown of a relationship, can result in a period of strong, volatile and variable emotions. This is a difficult and uncomfortable time. Although it is quite normal to have this type of reaction, and you cannot really avoid it altogether, the aim should be to reduce the severity of your distress and shorten the duration of this challenging period if you can do so.

This does not mean that you should fight against the emotions you feel. You cannot start a war with your emotional state and expect to be the victor. Also, you cannot ignore your emotions and expect them to just disappear. The aim should be to recognise and validate your emotional reactions, but do what you can to avoid your emotional distress escalating.

One way to do this is to focus your attention and coping efforts on your presenting emotional state. For example, if you feel sad then give this emotion your attention and work on ways to cope with your sadness. The sadness you are feeling is your primary emotion at that time. It is the emotion you feel directly because of what has happened to you.

It sounds straightforward. However, human beings are complex creatures who have the capacity to make themselves feel even more miserable. We experience different secondary emotions as a result of our reaction to the primary emotion. Let's consider how this might work with your sad feelings about the loss of your relationship.

What happened?	*My relationship ended.*
How do you feel?	*I feel sad* (primary emotion).
How do you react to the sadness?	*I don't like feeling sad, and I want it to go away.*
What do you say to yourself?	*"What if I can't stop being sad, and the feeling never goes away?"* *"What if I feel like this forever?"* *"What if I never recover?"*
What do you feel then?	*I feel fearful and anxious* (secondary emotion).
How do you react to the fear?	*I don't like the feeling, and I want it to go away.*

What do you say to yourself?	*"Now I feel anxious, and I can't cope."* *"I am stupid for feeling anxious when there is nothing to be afraid of."*
What do you feel then?	*I feel self-critical* (secondary emotion).
How do you react to this feeling?	*I feel uncomfortable and stressed.*
What do you say to yourself?	*"I am hopeless for feeling this way."*
What do you feel then?	*I feel annoyed with myself* (secondary emotion).

So now, instead of only feeling sadness, you feel sad, fearful, self-critical and annoyed. Your primary emotion of sadness was directly related to the problem situation that triggered the emotional reaction. The secondary emotions of fearfulness, a feeling of self-criticism and annoyance all developed as a result of your reaction to the primary emotion, that is, your sadness.

Your emotional reactions can be difficult to manage because what started as a straightforward emotional response to a stressful event turns into a confusing array of emotions. Sometimes, these emotions can compete with each other and pull you in different directions. For example, you can feel both sad and angry or angry and excited. Trying to deal with one of these emotions can be undermined by your efforts to deal with the other emotion.

There is a need to simplify things when you are dealing with difficult life events. You can learn to focus on your primary emotions as they arise and adopt strategies to deal with them. Let's start by looking at a way to identify your emotions so you know to what you should be giving your attention.

Recognising and dealing with your emotions

Let's start by taking the process of experiencing an emotional reaction a step at a time.

What happened?

Here, consider the situation that developed that resulted in you feeling these strong emotions. This might be the big, overriding problem (i.e., the breakdown of your relationship), or it might be a smaller aspect of the problem.

Why did this situation occur?

Consider the possible causes of the problem situation. This is an important step. It gives you the opportunity to interpret the meaning of the problem situation in an effort to help you understand why you are feeling the strong emotions you are experiencing.

How were you feeling as a result of that situation?

Try to identify your primary emotional response to the situation and then consider the secondary emotions you experience as well.

What is it that you wanted to do *as a result of how you were feeling?*

Here we are referring to the urges or impulses you have to act in response to the emotional state you are in. When feeling strong emotions, people tend to experience urges to do more extreme actions.

It does not follow that you will always do these things, however, thoughts about doing them can be present. It is worth noting that people tend to *think* about doing extreme things much more often than they ever *do* them. What this means is that you control the impulse to act in a 'over the top' way. If you can control these impulses, you can control others in a way that will allow you to have a more settled and reasonable response to provoking situations.

What did you actually do *and* say*?*

Here, you are considering what you actually did rather than what you had an urge to do.

After experiencing those emotions and actions, how did they affect you?

Here, we are referring to the consequences for you of experiencing those strong emotional states and your reactions to those states by choosing to act in a particular way.

Let's apply this strategy to the worksheet example below.

Understanding your emotions worksheet - example
Time and date: *Thursday 4th.*
What happened? *John told me he wanted to end our relationship. He then packed a bag and left.*
Why did this situation occur? *John wanted to pursue a new relationship with someone he met through work.*
How were you feeling as a result of that situation? *I felt devastated* (primary emotion), *and then I felt fearful, worthless and regretful* (secondary emotions).
What is it that you wanted to do as a result of how you were feeling? *I just wanted to pack up my things and move away to somewhere no one knew me.*
What did you actually do and say? *I burst into tears and pleaded with John not to leave.*
After experiencing those emotions and actions, how did they affect you? *After John left, I felt exhausted and overwhelmed and had a disturbed night. I wished I had not pleaded with John to stay.*

Let's examine another example of a different aspect of this relationship problem.

Understanding your emotions worksheet
Time and date: *Friday 19th.*
What happened? *John came around to collect some of his possessions, and an argument developed.*
Why did this situation occur? *The argument broke out because John believed I had hidden some of his things, so he couldn't take them.*
How were you feeling as a result of that situation? *I felt anger* (primary emotion) *and then I felt disappointed, confused and vengeful* (secondary emotions).
What is it that you wanted to do as a result of how you were feeling? *I wanted to just go and dump all his things in the closest rubbish bin.*
What did you actually do and say? *I yelled at John, "How dare you accuse me of hiding your stuff" and then I told him to leave.*
After experiencing those emotions and actions, how did they affect you? *I wandered around the house, looking for anything John had left behind. I ended up having a sleepless night, then had to face a day at work the next day feeling exhausted.*

To try and make sense of what you are feeling and why you are feeling it, we suggest you use the worksheet below. It is designed to help you to understand how you are reacting to the problems you are facing and this may direct you to how you can cope with the situation.

Understanding your emotions worksheet
Time and date:
What happened?
Why did this situation occur?
How were you feeling as a result of that situation?
What is it that you wanted to do as a result of how you were feeling?
What did you actually do and say?
After experiencing those emotions and actions, how did they affect you?

Worksheet available at elemen.com.au

The link between your emotions and your behaviour

It is worthwhile to understand the link between your emotional state and the things you choose to do in response to that emotion. This is important. It is difficult to control your behaviour choices if you do not appreciate the link between how you feel and what you do.

Let's consider how you might behave in relation to your emotional responses. Consider this example.

I felt	What I did
Sad	*I withdrew from everyone and hid away at home. I just curled up in a ball and allowed myself to be overcome by my sadness.*
Angry	*I sent my former partner some really nasty text messages and left them some horrible voicemail messages.*

Understanding this link between your emotional state and your behaviour can help you learn to make different choices in how you act when you are upset. We will explore this further when we consider building your coping strategies, but let's consider here how you might opt to do things differently. Consider the same example but now let's look at how this person might have chosen an alternative behaviour.

I felt	What I did	What I could have done instead
Sad	*I withdrew from everyone and hid away at home. I just curled up in a ball and allowed myself to be overcome by my sadness.*	*I could have reached out to my family and friends to talk over with them how I was feeling and ask their advice about what I should do.*
Angry	*I sent my former partner some really nasty text messages and left them some horrible voicemail messages.*	*When I felt angry, I could have distracted myself with an activity that would have soothed me and waited until the anger had passed.*

Let's take this one step further and consider the likely outcomes of the initial behaviour choice and the alternative one.

I felt…	*Sad.*
I did…	*I withdrew from everyone and hid away at home. I just curled up in a ball and allowed myself to be overcome by my sadness.*
What happened?	*I felt miserable for the rest of the day. I just couldn't shake it off. I turned down an invitation from a friend to spend time together and probably missed out on a fun time because of that.*
A better choice…	*I could have reached out to my family or a friend to talk over with them how I was feeling and ask their advice about what I should do.*
Likely outcome…	*I would have felt better much sooner. My family and friends would have helped me feel less sad. I would have joined in with what they were doing, and that would have distracted me and made me feel better.*
I felt…	*Angry.*
I did…	*I sent some really nasty text messages and left them some horrible voicemail messages.*
What happened?	*My former partner showed a friend the text messages and played the voicemail messages. That friend told me they were unhappy about what I had done. They said they didn't want to hear from me for a while.*
A better choice…	*When I felt angry, I could have distracted myself with an activity that would have soothed me and waited until the anger had passed.*
Likely outcome…	*My anger would have passed, and I would have felt better. I wouldn't have done anything that damaged my friendship.*

Initially, you can work on thinking up alternative and healthier behaviours after the event. This will allow you to learn how to make better choices by considering the different outcomes of various behaviours. It will then become easier to apply this strategy when you feel the emotional reaction so that you can choose the better behaviour at the time and avoid doing things that might feel all right at the time but do not help you in the longer term. Below is a worksheet you can use.

The emotion-behaviour link worksheet	
I feel/felt…	
I did/I felt the urge to do…	
What happened/ what would have happened?	
A better choice…	
Likely outcome…	

Worksheet available at elemen.com.au

Here you have learned to identify your emotional reactions and to respond to them differently, focusing on your primary emotions and responding to your urges to act in a different way.

It might be worthwhile next to give some additional assistance with the particularly difficult emotional response of anger. As this is the emotion that drives many of our poor behaviour choices, it is sensible to learn some additional skills.

Managing your anger

It should be noted that there are times when your increased nervous system arousal will manifest as an angry response rather than an anxious one. You might find yourself raising your voice or becoming overwhelmed by frustration and annoyance. You might act out in ways that you would not do if you were in a calmer state of mind. Certainly, at these times, you can act in a way that does not make you feel good about yourself when you reflect on what you have done.

If you have a more significant anger control problem, then we recommend that you seek a workbook that focuses on more extensive ways in which you can learn to control your anger or seek out professional help. However, here we would like to focus on some simple ideas that may help you control your angry feelings. Firstly, we will teach you a simple strategy to manage an angry response.

To understand why this strategy is effective, you need to consider that anger tends to be experienced in an escalating manner. That is, an angry response is triggered and then gets worse when one or both of two things happen. The first is that you can think anger-provoking thoughts that will build your anger. These thoughts tend to relate to things not being the way you want them to be and your feeling that what you are experiencing is not justified and should not be happening.

The second refers to a process of reaction to how the other person responds to your anger that escalates the angry interaction. That is, an initial angry comment can be made, and the other person then becomes angry, so you become more angry, and then the other person's anger increases further. This escalating pattern leads to uncontrolled anger.

So, what should you do if you find your anger being triggered or escalating?

Exit and wait strategy

The most straightforward strategy you can use to stop the escalation of your anger and allow it to abate is an exit and wait strategy. When you are feeling angry, leave the situation and wait until you are calm before you return. It is an easy and effective strategy. Walk out of the room and allow yourself to calm down.

When away from the anger-provoking situation, there are a couple of tips you can use to help you calm down more quickly. Firstly, avoid going over the angry situation in your mind. This only aggravates your anger and makes it harder for you to settle down. So, when you leave the room, try to think about something else. Distract yourself by focusing on something that will hold your attention. Secondly, you can physically control your angry reaction by slowing your breathing and relaxing your tense muscles. This allows you to bring your nervous system over-arousal under control.

When you are calm and better able to handle the situation, return to what you were doing when the angry response was triggered. Go back with the right frame of mind. Decide that you are going to disengage from the interaction that caused the problem. You can adopt a spectator role by simply observing what you are doing without interpreting and judging. This will help you to continue while reducing the risk of further escalations of anger.

Controlling thoughts that trigger anger

While the exit and wait technique is an emergency control strategy, you may need something more complex to effectively deal with your angry feelings. We can start by examining the types of thoughts that trigger angry feelings.

In a general sense, angry thoughts are triggered by a particular point of view that serves to justify our right to be angry. This point of view is made up of the following thought combination:

> I have been harmed or victimised by the other person.
>
> This person harmed me or victimised me deliberately.
>
> This person should not have done this; they were wrong; they should have chosen to act differently and in a way that would not harm or victimise me.

These thoughts tend to underlie most angry interactions. If you broke your angry thoughts into their particular elements, you would be able to discern the following:

> The harm done.
>
> The way it was done deliberately.
>
> Why this was wrong.

However, it should be remembered that this is your *perception* of the situation rather than the *facts* of the situation. How right or wrong you are in your perception is not determined by what you see as your justifiable anger. That is, your anger does not make these things true. Rightness or wrongness will be determined by the facts of the matter.

Unfortunately, it is hard to consider the facts when you are in an angry state. In effect, you are blinded by your emotional state and not in a position to think things through clearly.

Also, even if it is the case that someone has done the wrong thing, it does not mean that you cannot choose what way you will respond to this. It does not follow that you have to feel anger in response to someone else's actions. For example, you may choose to just shrug your shoulders about their behaviour and ignore their attempts to rile you. You may feel disappointed the person acted in the way they did but feel determined to rise above their poor behaviour.

Instead of just focusing on the situation that triggered your anger, you may be better served to think of ways that would allow you to control how you respond. This allows you to take responsibility for the outcome rather than being a helpless victim of someone else's poor behaviour. Consider the following example.

Changing my reaction – Example 1

What happened to provoke my anger?

Eric came into the house when I wasn't there to collect some things. He made himself a snack, watched television and left his plate and mug on the coffee table for me to clean up.

How did I interpret this event?

I interpreted this as Eric taking advantage of me... eating my food, and expecting me to clean up after him. I believed that Eric did it deliberately to provoke me, so he could then say I was the unreasonable one.

What did I think should happen?

I think Eric should have contacted me and made an arrangement to come and collect his things rather than enter what is now my home without my permission.

How could I think differently about this situation?

I could see this experience as a trigger for me following through with my decision to either have Eric return the house keys or to have the locks changed.

How is this likely to make me feel?

This would make me feel more in control and better protected from these types of things happening in the future. I would feel relieved that Eric could not just walk into my home whenever he wanted.

Let's consider another example.

Changing my reaction – Example 2
What happened to provoke my anger? *Kirsten told some people we both know that I was the one to blame for the end of the relationship. She told them I was the one to leave because I was interested in someone else.*
How did I interpret this event? *I believed this was her attempt to shift the blame to me so that our friends would side with her. She was trying to ruin my friendships.*
What did I think should happen? *I think she should have been honest and said she was the one who ended the relationship. I think she should not have interfered with my friendships and got people to side with her.*
How could I think differently about this situation? *I could remind myself that the people who really matter to me will talk to me about what happened rather than simply taking Kirsten's word. In the end, this is likely to cause Kirsten embarrassment when people realise she is not telling the truth. If other people believe her, well... that is their right, I suppose, but they are not my true friends. I would rather spend time with true friends.*
How is this likely to make me feel? *This would make me feel calmer because I wouldn't be so worried about the impact of what she is doing. I don't think I would care nearly as much if I realised this is unlikely to have any real impact on my true friendships.*

It is a good idea for you to work through your reactions to anger-provoking situations to see if you can re-interpret them in a way that helps you control your angry feelings. It is worth keeping in mind that angry feelings can be unpleasant and can drive you to do things that you might not choose to do if you were calmer. You can use the worksheet below to go through this process of reframing your response to anger-provoking situations.

Changing my reaction worksheet
What happened to provoke my anger?
How did I interpret this event?
What did I think should happen?
How could I think differently about this situation?
How is this likely to make me feel?

Worksheet available at elemen.com.au

If your angry reactions are just a reflection of the situation you are in, then these steps may help you manage those reactions and help you choose to react differently and in a way that is advantageous to you. This can help you settle your nervous system and feel more in control. Certainly, without reactive anger, you can begin to think differently and more clearly about your situation.

Learning acceptance

To cope with overwhelming emotional states, such as those caused by the breakdown of an important relationship, it is necessary to learn ways to manage the distress you feel when stressful things happen.

A change of attitude

Typically, when stressful events occur, we react to them in the context of something being done to us or happening to us. If we hold someone else responsible, then we tend to react with anger and resentment, holding the view that the person involved should have done something other than what they did. If we hold ourselves responsible, then we tend to focus on self-criticism and regret. The result is that we start a battle within ourselves in relation to the event. The more we focus on our anger and resentment, or our self-criticism and regret, the more distressed we tend to feel in relation to our experiences that triggered these feelings.

The trouble with this approach is that it does not really let us accept and deal with the fact that the event has actually happened and that we must cope with it… because we have little choice. We focus more on the past, which we cannot change, and give less attention to the present and the future, over which we can exert some control.

When you are dealing with the breakdown of your relationship, you are faced with ongoing challenges. Most of these challenges are not things you would choose to have happen. This can cause you to experience distress when the challenges occur and even after they occur.

To cope with this, you need to consider a change in attitude to one of acceptance rather than being tormented by events that you cannot change. There are lots of things that can happen that cause you pain and emotional upset. The more you focus on these situations, the more distress you tend to feel. The goal here is to learn to accept the things you cannot change.

Often when we have to deal with a change we did not want, we tend to get upset thinking that this is something that should not have happened or should not have happened to you in particular. Rather than battle events that have already occurred in this way, the goal is to accept that they *did* happen and it is now appropriate for you to deal with these changed circumstances.

Being distressed about a situation does not help you cope with that situation. It is a fact that you cannot change the past. Nevertheless, we tend to emotionally react to these situations as if there is something we can do to change them. In doing this, you become stuck and do not look for other, more effective ways of coping with your new circumstance.

In learning acceptance, you need to acknowledge your changed situation without trying to control it or change things that have already happened. Try to understand that your current situation has occurred because there was a long chain of events that occurred in the past that brought you to this point. Your job now is to use your coping skills to move forward with life as it is a waste of your energy and effort to torment yourself thinking "if only…" or "what if…".

This type of acceptance does not mean that you cannot wish that things had turned out differently. It also does not stop you from looking for ways to manage or improve your current situation or avoid things that might happen in the future. This type of acceptance is asking you to look at your situation and accept it for what it is. It is from here that you can then choose what you want to do about it.

Whenever you feel overwhelmed by your situation, you can use simple coping statements that will remind you that a position of acceptance is preferable. Consider the following coping statements. Add any that you can think of that would help you accept what has happened so that you can move forward and deal with things as they arise.

Acceptance coping statements
Below are some examples of coping statements that would help you achieve acceptance. These coping statements remind you to accept your situation and the events that contributed to your current situation. Tick the coping statements that you would find useful, and then add any others you believe will help. Then, when you feel overwhelmed, use these coping statements to help you manage your reaction to the events that are stressing you.

	Things are the way they are.
	There is a chain of things that contributed to what is happening now.
	I cannot change things that have already happened.
	There is no point battling past events.
	Battling the past upsets my present.
	I can only deal with the present.
	It is a waste of my energy to try to change the past.
	The present is as it should be, even if it is not what I would choose.
	This moment in time has occurred because of all the things that came before.

Add your own coping statements	

Checklist available at elemen.com.au

These coping statements can remind you to stop fighting a past you cannot change. This will free you up to accept what has happened and then focus your energy on moving forward and doing what is best for you. Acceptance of what has happened invites you to cope with what you are experiencing.

Using effective coping strategies

We have already covered information about coping preferences and coping strategies, both good ones and ones that do not work very effectively. We are now going to consider how to take full advantage of your ways of coping, building on problem-approach strategies and letting go of problem-avoidance strategies.

Building your coping repertoire

As you now better understand the ways you cope, you can start to build a plan of how you are going to move forward, adopting coping strategies that work for you. Let's consider some examples of coping strategies you could adopt.

Problem-focused strategies

We will start by looking at problem-solving strategies. Here you are trying to work out a plan of how you would go about solving a specific problem situation, followed by decision-making with regard to which potential solution you would choose. You then should be able to follow through and solve your problem.

Let's consider an example of this process.

Example of a problem-solving strategy
What is the problem? Clearly define the problem you are facing. *This is my home and I don't want to leave but it is very expensive to live here by myself and I can't afford it.*
Generate as many possible solutions as you can. List the ones that are likely to work. *I could do the following:* *I could cut down on other expenses and continue to live here.* *I could continue to live here by finding a housemate to share expenses.* *I could move and find somewhere else to live that I could comfortably afford.*

Consider the likelihood of each of these strategies being successful.

The likely outcomes are:

> *If I cut down my expenses so that I could continue to live here, I would probably find myself having financial difficulty. Although it might seem like a good option, in reality, I would find myself so stretched financially that I would not be able to afford to live comfortably. Also, I would probably find myself with additional bills (e.g., if my car broke down or needed new tyres) that I would really struggle to be able to pay. I would be constantly worried about money.*
>
> *Getting a housemate makes sense, in theory. I could charge that person rent and additional bills, such as electricity, would be shared. However, I just can't imagine being happy living with someone else. It would feel like a real intrusion and it wouldn't suit my need for space and peace and quiet.*

I really don't want to move. However, I could find somewhere that I liked that was within my financial means and allowed me to have extra income to spend on other things... both necessary things as well as some fun things. In addition, I know I could make a new place my own... put my own touches on it and make it comfortable for me. It would feel like it was truly mine and a fresh start.

Select the problem-solving strategy that is likely to work the best.

I think I will choose to move. Not because I really want to but because it is the option that is most likely to work out well for me. The other options have significant problems with them that would be either hard to overcome or difficult to live with. I know I can make myself a comfortable home that feels like mine if I decide to move.

What are you going to do next?

I am going to start to give some serious thought to what area I would like to live in. I might visit some areas to see what they are like. I will also start to look at real estate websites to see what is available. If I am going to move, I want the move to be a good one to somewhere I can get excited about.

In this example, the person has thought about the problem and identified possible options for resolving it. The person then considered what the likely outcome for each possible solution would be. They then chose their preferred solution and worked out a plan for their next step. This is a good problem-solving approach.

Below is a worksheet you can use for problem-solving coping strategies.

A problem-solving strategy worksheet
What is the problem? Clearly define the problem you are facing.
Generate as many possible solutions as you can. List the ones that are likely to work.
Consider the likelihood of each of these strategies being successful.
Select the problem-solving strategy that is likely to work the best.
What are you going to do next?

Worksheet available at elemen.com.au

Now, let's consider a cognitive restructuring approach to coping. Cognitive restructuring refers to changing the way you are thinking about a problem. Below is an example of a cognitive restructuring approach to addressing a problem situation.

Example of a cognitive restructuring strategy
What is the problem? *My so-called friend uninvited me from a dinner party. They told me it was 'only for couples' and I would feel uncomfortable being there by myself.*
What are you thinking? *I am going to lose all my friends because I am single.*
What evidence do you have that this is true? *Well... there was this one time when a friend uninvited me from the dinner party.*
What evidence do you have against this being true? *I have been flooded with invitations from friends to do things with them. Some of these people have been in the same situation as me in the past and understand what I am going through. These people, in particular, have been in regular contact, including the ones who now have new relationships.*
Even if it was true, what is the worst thing that would happen? *Even if it happened that I lost all my friends, I would still have the opportunity to make new ones. Although it seems unlikely that I would lose all my friends, I am able to meet new people and form friendships.*
What do you conclude? *I think I have been worrying about nothing. One person who didn't want a single person to attend her dinner party rudely uninvited me. Lots of other people have gone out of their way to include me, even with their family events. I think I was just hurt by that person's behaviour and blew it out of proportion.*

Here, the person in this example challenged the way they were thinking about their situation. Then, they examined whether the situation was as bad as they were interpreting it to be. Having realised that was not the case, they then worked out a better and more realistic way of thinking about their problem. You can see that their alternative thoughts about their situation would make it easier for them to cope. They had been tormented by thoughts that they would be rejected. Instead, by working through the situation, they were able to see that they had overreacted to the hurtful and rude behaviour of one person.

Below is a worksheet you can use for cognitive restructuring strategies.

A cognitive restructuring strategy worksheet
What is the problem?
What are you thinking?
What evidence do you have that this is true?
What evidence do you have against this being true?
Even if it was true, what is the worst thing that would happen?
What do you conclude?

Worksheet available at elemen.com.au

Emotion-focused strategies

Next, we will consider how to enhance your emotion expression coping skills.

Example of an emotion expression strategy
What is the problem? *I didn't want people to know that my relationship had ended.*
What did you do? *I chose not to tell anyone my relationship was over except for my closest family members.*
What were the advantages of doing this? *With people not knowing, they didn't ask me how I was doing. In this way, I didn't have to talk about it.*
What were the disadvantages of doing this? *I couldn't talk about it even if I wanted to. I couldn't talk to someone and just let my bottled up feelings go. I have been going to work and pretending that everything is ok and that has been really hard, hiding how I have been feeling. There have been times when I have felt really lonely and overwhelmed but I couldn't talk to my friends to express how I have been feeling.*
What could you have done differently? *I could have told my friends and workmates what has happened but told them there might be times when I wanted to talk about it but times when I didn't want to talk.*
What would the advantages have been of doing things this other way? *I would have felt like I wasn't carrying around this huge secret so I would have felt relieved. I would have had friends available to talk to about how I was feeling when things were too much for me to cope with. This would have allowed me the opportunity to express how I was feeling in a genuine way. I could have got some understanding from my employer and workmates. This would have allowed me to be sad at work if that was how I felt.*
Would there have been any disadvantage of doing things this other way? *Not really. People would know about my relationship, but I see now that it wouldn't be a disadvantage.*

> What will you do next time you feel like this?
>
> *Next time I see someone I haven't told, I will just tell them. If I feel sad or lonely, I will just admit to that. This will allow me to not feel all bottled up.*

In this case, the person went through a process of examining the pros and cons associated with the decision they made to not tell anyone about the end of their relationship. They recognised that this had prevented them from genuinely expressing their emotions in a way that would have been a relief for them. The conclusion was reached that the better option was to allow themselves to react in a genuine way to what they were feeling by telling people what had happened so that they did not have to pretend to be all right when they did not feel that way.

Below is a worksheet for emotion expression strategies.

An emotion expression strategy worksheet
What is the problem?
What did you do?
What were the advantages of doing this?
What were the disadvantages of doing this?
What could you have done differently?

What would the advantages have been of doing things this other way?
Would there have been any disadvantage of doing things this other way?
What will you do next time you feel like this?

Worksheet available at elemen.com.au

Finally, we can consider how to use social support as a coping strategy.

Example of social support as a strategy
What is the problem? *There have been times when I have felt really lonely and isolated.*
What have you done in response to this problem? *Whenever I have felt lonely and isolated, I have just curled up in bed and tried to sleep to pass the time and avoid having to deal with how I have been feeling.*
How has responding in this way helped you with your problem? *It hasn't really helped at all. After laying in bed, I get up and still feel lonely.*
What could you do instead? *When I feel like that, I can reach out to family and friends.*
How would this be likely to work out? *I know my family and true friends care about me and would do what they could to help. We wouldn't have to talk about the relationship ending all the time. It would sometimes just be nice to be around people talking about and doing ordinary things. This would make me feel much better... not as lonely or isolated.*

> So, what are you going to do next?
>
> *Next time I feel like this, I am going to phone a family member or friend... either just to talk or to arrange to do something that I would enjoy.*

Here, the person thought through their situation and realised they were doing the opposite of what they should have been doing to fix their problem of loneliness. They realised the solution was available to them and there were advantages to pursuing the solution. It was an easy step then to follow through with their plan and reach out to others.

Below is a worksheet you can use for social support strategies.

A social support as a strategy worksheet
What is the problem?
What have you done in response to this problem?
How has responding in this way helped you with your problem?
What could you do instead?
How would this be likely to work out?
So, what are you going to do next?

Worksheet available at elemen.com.au

In moving forward, remember to choose the coping strategies that best suit your preferred coping style. Always choose approach strategies rather than avoidance strategies, no matter what your coping style.

Thinking your way to less distress

So far in this workbook, we have indicated that the way we think about the things we experience influences how we react to them. We have touched on this when we considered learning to accept what has happened, learning to regulate your emotions, and learning to control angry feelings, in particular. To feel better, we might have to change the way we view something so that we are not vulnerable to distressed reactions to events that have already happened and we cannot control. Let's now consider other ways we can challenge unhelpful thinking and replace it with the types of thoughts that allow us to see things more clearly and choose behaviours that will help us.

How are our thoughts affected?

As we go through life, we can develop unhelpful thinking styles or errors in our thinking. These errors influence how we interpret the world around us and how we fit into that world. In an attempt to make sense of the world, we develop 'templates' or models of how we think things should work.

For example, you might develop a template that tells you that to be a worthwhile person, everyone should like you. On the surface, this seems workable. It is nice when people like you, and it makes you feel good, including feeling good about yourself. However, if you have a template that you are worthwhile only if everyone likes you, what happens if, for some reason, someone chooses not to like you? You then become upset about something that really is an ordinary enough experience. You then feel like you are not worthwhile, even in situations where the fact that the other person does not like you says more about them than it does about you. We have found that people choose not to like others for the oddest of reasons. For example, one person disclosed that they found they could not like people who even vaguely looked like a cousin they did not admire. Should your feelings of self-worth be affected by the fact that you look somewhat like a person you have never met? It is obvious that the answer is no. Unfortunately, your template might tell you that to be a worthwhile person, *everyone* has to like you. You can see the problem.

Our individual templates are put together based on information from a variety of sources, including, for example, our personality and our experiences throughout life. If the messages we receive from our experiences in life are good and healthy ones, we tend to have good and healthy templates of how the world works and how we fit into that world. However, if the messages are distorted in some way (e.g., being told you have to be the best at everything you do, that no one will like you if you disagree with them, your needs are not as important as other people's needs), then the template we develop will reflect these messages and will be unhelpful.

Core beliefs

So, how does this template affect us? It tells us how we should respond when dealing with our world and the people in it. The information we gather determines our 'core beliefs' about three things:

>How safe or dangerous we perceive the world to be.

>Our place in that world and our value as a person.

>How certain the future feels.

These core beliefs are not the 'truth' of things. They develop as a result of the information we gather along the way in life, whether or not that information is helpful or unhelpful, clear or confusing, or accurate or distorted.

If we have helpful, clear and accurate templates, then our core beliefs are healthy, and our thinking does not contain errors about how the world works and how we fit into that world. However, if we have unhelpful, confusing and distorted templates, our thinking contains errors that affect how we react to the world and how we view ourselves in that world.

Cognitive errors

Cognitive errors are the errors in thinking that occur when our templates of how the world works and how we fit into that world send us the wrong message. Our thinking about our experiences is then altered by the wrong message. Problems arise when we engage in certain types of cognitive errors.

Below are some of the most common cognitive errors. As you read through them, think about whether these types of errors occur in your thinking.

Table 6: Descriptions of the common errors in thinking.

Types of errors in thinking	
Error type	*Error in thinking*
Filtering	A person whose thinking is affected by filtering takes the negative details of an event and exaggerates them while filtering out any positive aspects about the situation. For example, a person who has been offered considerable support from family and friends after the breakdown of their relationship may ignore the meaning of these offers and focus only on one person's expressed view that they were not willing to offer support.

Polarised thinking	With polarised thinking, things are either 'black or white' or 'all or nothing'. People who think this way place situations in 'either/or' categories, with no middle ground to account for the complexity of most situations. For example, a person may view themselves as lovable, as evidenced by being in a relationship, or entirely unlovable, as evidenced by their relationship being over.
Overgeneralisation	A person makes a conclusion based on one event or a single piece of information. In this way, if something bad happens to them on one occasion, they expect it to happen over and over again. For example, a person may form the view that because one relationship failed, they will be unsuccessful in all relationships.
Jumping to conclusions	If a person jumps to conclusions, they 'know' what the other person is thinking about without that person saying so. For example, a person whose partner left their relationship believes that others think they are at fault despite no one ever saying so.
Catastrophising	A person who catastrophises expects disaster to strike, no matter what. A person hears about a problem and uses *what-if* questions to imagine the worst outcome. For example, a person entering into a property settlement negotiation after the end of their relationship may predict that they will end up with nothing while their ex-partner takes everything they owned.
Personalisation	A person believes that everything others do or say is some kind of direct, personal reaction to them. They take everything personally. For example, a passing comment by someone at a social engagement that people are better off not staying in a poor relationship is taken by this person as a comment that their former partner, in particular, was right to abandon them.

Control fallacies	This occurs when a person strongly endorses the view that they must be in control of all situations or control is being exerted on them. This can occur in two ways. Firstly, there is external control where the person feels they are a helpless victim of fate or, secondly, internal control where a person assumes responsibility for the pain and unhappiness of others. For example, a person might feel overwhelming guilt because they were the cause of their former partner's unhappiness even though the former partner does not blame them for the decisions the former partner made.
Fallacy of fairness	A person who believes they know what is fair will feel resentful and unhappy if others disagree with them. People who judge every event in their lives in terms of whether or not it is fair will often feel resentful, angry and hopeless. For example, a person may see it as unfair that their relationship failed because they had done everything they considered right and necessary to make a relationship work.
Blaming	This person holds other people responsible for their own emotional pain. Alternatively, they may blame themselves for every problem – even those clearly outside their control. For example, a person may hold him or herself responsible for their former partner meeting someone else and falling in love even though they played no part in that process.
Shoulds	Should statements (e.g., I should visit my parents more) are made by people who hold rigid rules about how the world should work and how everyone should behave. Breaking these rules makes a person angry. They also feel guilty when they violate their own rules. For example, a person may believe they should take advice when it is offered but then be pulled in different directions by the incompatibility of the advice they are given by various people.
Emotional reasoning	People with this distortion in thinking are guided by what they 'feel' is the truth. They will rely on their feelings to establish whether or not something is 'fact'. If a person feels stupid and boring, then they must be stupid and boring. Emotional reasoning blocks rationality and logic. For example, a person who, after a relationship ending, feels unlovable and believes this is evidence that they are unlovable.

Fallacy of change	A person with this type of thinking will believe that if they apply enough pressure, others will change to meet their needs. This person needs others to change because they cannot cope if others disagree with them or behave in ways that are contrary to how this person feels they should behave. For example, a person whose partner left them might believe they can change their partner's mind if they put enough pressure on them to do so.
Global labelling	A person generalises a small number of features or characteristics of themselves or others and inflates them into a global statement or judgment. This goes beyond overgeneralising. Rather than take into account the context of a situation, the person will apply this judgment to all aspects of a person or situation. For example, because a partner ended a relationship, a person might believe they are a worthless and unlovable person that no one would want to commit themselves to.
Always being right	When a person engages in this error of thinking, they insist that all views held by them or actions done by them are correct. In their view, they cannot make a mistake or be misinformed. For example, a person who believes that friends always 'pick a side after a relationship ends and who always has to be right may pressure their friends to take their side to prove themselves right.
Heaven's reward fallacy	A person who engages in this type of thinking believes that a person's hard work and sacrifice will pay off in the end, as if someone is keeping track of what everyone does in life. Sharing some similarities with the fallacy of fairness thinking, this person believes that the one who does the most or, works the hardest or sacrifices the most will be the person who is rewarded at some point in the future. For example, a person may be confused about the end of a relationship because they believe they are a good person who tried hard to do everything right. How can bad things happen to someone who tries so hard to be good?

Let's consider how these errors in thinking affect a person's point of view. Below are examples of these types of logical errors in thinking, along with a more rational point of view.

Table 7: Examples of rational and irrational perspectives for each error in thinking.

Correcting your thinking	
Error in thinking	*A rational view*
Filtering	
Joel's family and friends reassured him that he had done all he could to make the relationship work and he was right to have made the decision to end the relationship. In contrast, one acquaintance said he had not tried hard enough and had failed his partner by not meeting her needs. Joel only focused on what this acquaintance said to him. He concluded that he had not made the right decision, and he should have done more to care for his partner.	In general, Joel should be confident about the decision he made to end a relationship that was not working after he had tried to do what he could to rectify the problem. The majority of people who offered an opinion supported Joel's decision. Only one person who does not know him as well as others offered a different opinion. Joel should have looked at all the information available to him and reached a conclusion that others thought he had done his best rather than focus on the dissenting opinion.
Polarised thinking	
Sean had a good relationship history. He had one relationship when he was young that ended as their lives took different pathways when they left uni. His second relationship was a close and loving one that ended when his partner accepted a job overseas. His most recent relationship, in contrast, ended badly. His partner accused him of not meeting her needs and the relationship ended with considerable animosity on his part and hers. Sean formed the view that, because of this failed relationship, he was not relationship material. He could not imagine himself being in a successful relationship. He thought he should just accept he would not have a good relationship in the future.	Sean should have considered this one failed relationship in the context of his overall relationship history. In effect, it is possible for everyone to have failed relationships, so that, in itself, would not indicate that Sean could not maintain a relationship. Sean should have focused on a less polarised view and seen that one relationship failure would not define his future.

Overgeneralisation	
Sonya was in a relationship with Finn. Finn was stressed because of work and was more irritable than usual. Finn snapped at Sonya because of some minor things that annoyed him. Sonya became upset and Finn became frustrated so an argument developed. Sonya formed the view that her relationship with Finn was never going to work because they had failed to communicate well on this one occasion. Sonya ended the relationship with Finn, seeing no point in trying to work things out.	Sonya would have done well to consider that one minor incident in the context of other positive experiences with her boyfriend did not warrant a conclusion that their relationship would never work. Rather than this one argument reflecting an overall pattern of dysfunction and poor communication in the relationship, it probably demonstrated nothing more than the fact that people become more irritable if they have had a bad day.
Jumping to conclusions	
Olivia's partner had left the relationship because he no longer wanted to be responsible for parenthood and a housing loan. His unmarried mates had a more carefree lifestyle that Olivia's partner also wanted. Despite Olivia's family and friends understanding that this was her partner's decision and their acceptance of her explanation for his decision, Olivia believed that her family and friends thought that the breakdown of the relationship was Olivia's fault. She believed they thought she had not done enough to please her partner and this was the reason he left.	Rather than jump to a conclusion without any evidence this was the case, Olivia would have felt better if she had relied on the objective facts to which she had access. In this case, Olivia's family and friends had told her that they supported her and accepted that her partner had made a decision to end the relationship for the reasons stated. Without any evidence at all that they thought otherwise, it was serving Olivia no good purpose to believe they thought otherwise.

Catastrophising	
Poppy just knew that things were going to turn out badly. She knew that a division of assets after the end of her relationship was going to leave her unable to secure accommodation for herself despite it being likely that she would received a good amount of money and despite Poppy holding a highly paying job. Poppy kept thinking of the worst case scenario despite there being no evidence that this was likely to occur. No amount of reassurance by family, friends, her lawyer and even her ex-partner could make her feel better.	Poppy's anxiety was causing her, in effect, to make up a story in her mind that things were going to be disastrous and she would end up having nowhere to live. Poppy should have focused on the objective indicators of the likely outcome in her property settlement process rather than relying on her subjective feelings to influence how she viewed her likely future. Had she done this, she would have seen that there were much more likely outcomes than the terrible one she was predicting.

Personalisation	
Gemma's best friend had not been in touch for a couple of weeks after she had been so supportive in the initial period after Gemma's relationship ended. Gemma was aware that her friend's mother had been very ill and she had heard that her mother had been hospitalised recently. Despite this knowledge, Gemma believed that her friend had withdrawn because she had overburdened her with her need for support after her relationship broke down.	In reality, Gemma's friend had her own problems on which she needed to focus her attention. The simplest explanation, then, is that Gemma's friend's problems were causing her to have less time for her friend. Gemma would be better off realising that her friend's unavailability had nothing to do with her. This would have caused Gemma to feel less abandoned by her friend and, perhaps, more sympathetic with regard to her friend's own situation.

Control fallacies	
Warren thought he was unlucky in life. He thought that no matter what he did, the world was against him. He saw himself as a victim of some force that targeted him but not others who had a better life than Warren. Warren saw the end of his relationship as just another example of the world being against him and controlling his life and happiness.	With Warren holding the view that he had no control over how the world was treating him, he made no effort to exert any influence on how things worked out for him. He would have been better off considering the breakdown of his relationship as an event that happens to people and considering ways he could react to this event so that he felt more in control. He should have examined the objective influences on what occurred and given thought to how he could react differently and make different choices in the future.

Fallacy of fairness	
Leah had ended her relationship with Robert. The relationship was not offering her what she needed, and she wanted to move on with her life. Robert accepted her decision and set about moving on with his life. He accepted invitations from friends to do fun, social things. Leah was furious that Robert was not suffering more. She told her family and friends that it was not fair that Robert had seemingly been unaffected by the end of the relationship and was happy. Given that Leah did not want the relationship to continue and had been the person who ended it, her family and friends were confused by her attitude. According to Leah, it was only fair that Robert should suffer.	The fact of the matter is that sometimes, things do not work out the way we expect. In any case, these things are often unrelated to any sense of 'fairness'. Believing she can apply an understanding of fairness to decisions made by Robert is just making Leah unhappy for no real purpose. By accepting that Robert is free to do as he wishes, Leah would be able to focus on her own life and put effort and energy into the changes she wishes to make.

Blaming	
Audrey was overwhelmed by a sense of responsibility for the end of her relationship. Despite her husband leaving the relationship to pursue a relationship with someone else he had met through work, Audrey blamed herself. Audrey tormented herself by thoughts that the relationship would have survived if only she had done things differently. She did not know what it was that she should have done differently but she still held herself responsible for not doing these things.	Audrey blamed herself for decisions made by others even though she did not even know about these decisions until her husband informed her their relationship was over. It would have been more helpful for her to realise we are all responsible for our own conduct but not the conduct of others. She was holding herself accountable for the actions of others that were not known to her. This was making her feel even more stressed than was necessary. By accepting that she is not to blame and that sometimes things we do not want to happen nonetheless happen, Audrey would free herself to focus on what she needs now and in the future instead of being trapped in a past she cannot change.
Shoulds	
Dylan had always been of the view that if people took the time to give him advice, he should listen. After his wife ended their marriage, Dylan was inundated with advice. In fact, he was overwhelmed. The problem was that the advice he received was contradictory. Dylan was in a state of confusion because of his rigid rule that he should act on advice given to him. He felt pulled in multiple directions, and he did not know what to do. If he followed one person's advice, as he believed he should, then he was rejecting the advice of others.	Dylan's belief that he should follow people's advice was not working for him. His rule was too rigid, and he could not cope with the problem of conflicting advice. Dylan needed to adjust his rule to make it more flexible. For example, a rule that says he can consider advice that is both helpful and consistent with his own thoughts on the matter in question would allow Dylan to take advantage of the help offered by people while also comfortably rejecting the opinions of others that were unhelpful and inconsistent with the standards of behaviour he might set for himself.

Emotional reasoning	
After their relationship ended, Suzanne was convinced her husband was going to take everything and leave her unable to support herself. Suzanne had never coped well with insecurity. So, despite her husband's assurances that he had no intention of being unfair in the property settlement and would not act to take her share, Suzanne feared that is what would happen. As Suzanne's fear increased, she became increasingly convinced that this was what he would do. She told others that this was what he intended, and although they were shocked that he would act in a way that would harm her, given what they knew of him, they had no reason to doubt what she was saying. She certainly seemed frightened.	The intensity of Suzanne's fear of something happening convinced her that her fear was warranted. Suzanne was basing her reasoning on her emotional state rather than the more obvious indicators (e.g., her husband's reassurance, what everyone knew of the character of her husband). She was taking her emotional response and allowing it to influence her reasoning. She would have been better off waiting to see what would happen and then decide how she felt about it. Problem first, emotional reaction second – not the other way around.

Fallacy of change	
Lydia's ex-partner, Andrew, was never very comfortable talking about his feelings. Lydia had always known this about him. In contrast, Lydia loved to talk about how she was feeling and dissect every interaction she had with Andrew to understand its meaning. Lydia constantly pressured Andrew to engage in intense and exhausting discussions about how Andrew felt about even the tiniest things. In the end, Andrew ended the relationship for that and a variety of other reasons. Despite him being insistent that he did not wish to continue in the relationship, Lydia thought all their relationship problems would resolve if Andrew would just talk about how he was feeling. She continued to pressure Andrew to discuss things with her.	Lydia has made the mistake of assuming that because she values something, everyone else should value it, too. She is demanding that Andrew change to meet her needs. She is expecting Andrew to 'see sense' and stop withholding this from her. She fails to see that she is upsetting herself by expecting something the other person is not willing or able to provide.

Global labelling	
Brad was convinced he was hopeless and that he would fail at everything he undertook. Brad formed this view because his relationship with his girlfriend ended. She blamed Brad for the break-up, claiming he had failed to be the sort of person she was looking for. Brad formed the view that he just was not good enough and would repeatedly fail so there was no point trying.	Brad's upset emotional state is colouring the way he views himself in a global sense. Because one thing went wrong, everything must be terrible. Brad's girlfriend had her own views about who she was looking for in a boyfriend, and that influenced her decision about Brad's suitability for her. Brad then made the illogical leap to the view that he was worthless in all aspects of his life. Brad would be better off avoiding labelling himself in a global way about one event in his life.
Always being right	
Ian's friends were reasonable people. They realise that they can maintain their friendships with Ian and his former partner without any conflict. But that was not Ian's view. He was convinced that after the end of a relationship, people who were friendly with the couple must choose whose side they were on. His friends tried to reassure him this was not an issue, but Ian 'knew' otherwise. As a result of his belief that sides should be taken, and to prove that he was right in holding this view, Ian began placing considerable pressure on his friends to make a choice. He wanted each of them to declare they were on his side or, he told them, he could not expect their friendship to continue. In wanting to be proven correct, Ian was making things difficult for his friends and causing damage to his friendships.	Ian would have been better off realising that people may see things differently from him. Some people may choose sides, but others may not. However, Ian was losing friends, not because his relationship ended but because of the pressure he was placing on the people he cared about. It would have served him better to be more relaxed about the issue and allow people to make up their own minds about how they conduct themselves.

Heaven's reward fallacy	
Chloe always put other people's needs before her own. She ran around after people, she listened to their problems, she looked after their children and their pets. Recently, Chloe developed a problem of her own in that her relationship ended and she turned to her friends for support. She was surprised that they did not really take the amount of time she expected to listen to her problems and help her despite all of the effort she had put into caring for them. Chloe's feelings were hurt, and she was confused by her friends' failure to meet her needs at a time when she really needed their help.	Chloe made the mistake of believing that because she had done the right thing, other people would do the same. Everyone is driven by their own motivations. Each person sets the standard for their own behaviour. Although it would be nice if people reciprocated, there is simply no guarantee that will happen when you enter into an association with another person.

It is apparent that these types of logical errors do not make things easy for us. Quite the opposite. They lead us to misinterpret events so that we adopt a limited or negative perspective that colours how we view things, our emotional responses, and the choices of how we behave as a consequence.

Why do we think in unhelpful ways?

Why do we think in ways that are distorted and not particularly helpful? To understand why errors in thinking happen, we have to consider the theory behind cognitive behaviour therapy (CBT). According to this theory, our thinking has more than one level. This is displayed in the diagram below.

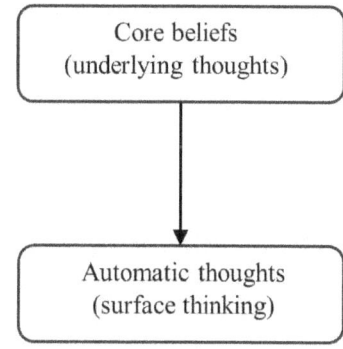

Figure 5: A diagram of the two levels of thought.

Automatic thoughts refer to the running commentary that goes through our heads as we go about our daily lives. If you pay attention, you will notice the constant chatter that goes on in your head about the things you are doing and how you are reacting to the people and events around you.

There is an easy exercise that will show you how this running commentary works. For the next minute, think about a bowl of fruit. Over the course of the minute, just let your thoughts do what they want as you think about a bowl of fruit. At the end of the minute, notice where your thoughts have taken you. Now consider the links between your starting point (thinking about a bowl of fruit) and where you ended up (thinking whatever it was you were thinking). Consider below how this might have played out for one individual. This person started thinking about a bowl of fruit and ended up thinking about cleaning out their pantry. Follow their automatic thoughts.

> *Ok. I'm thinking about a bowl of fruit. I can picture a bowl of fruit. It's got bananas in it. I like bananas. I should buy some next time I go to the supermarket. I also need to get a loaf of bread. I must start a shopping list. Pay attention and think about a bowl of fruit. Oh, and milk, I mustn't forget milk. I hate running out of milk. Someone said once that they have orange juice on their cereal instead of milk. Yuck. I couldn't imagine anything worse. Not that I eat much cereal. I should eat more cereal... it's probably good for you. I will put cereal on my shopping list. But that might be a waste because I probably won't eat it. I have bought lots of things I thought would be good for me, but I never ate them. That reminds me that I should clean out the pantry.*

In contrast to automatic thoughts, core beliefs refer to the underlying beliefs we have about how the world works and how we fit into that world. Core beliefs have influence on our automatic thoughts. That is, we think the things we do on the surface because of our underlying beliefs about how things work. Unlike automatic thoughts, the content of our core beliefs is not readily available to us but can be examined by considering the content of our automatic thoughts.

So, where do the logical errors in thinking we have been talking about fit into this conceptualisation? Let's consider that in the diagram below.

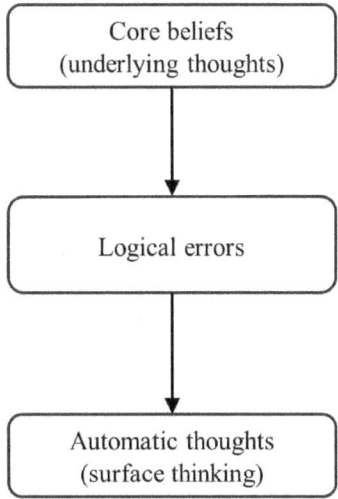

Figure 6: Where errors in thinking occur in our levels of thought.

The errors in thinking we make are a result of the core beliefs we hold. For example, if our core beliefs about the world and the future are that the world is threatening and the outlook is grim and pessimistic, then we are likely to inflate the degree of dangerousness we perceive and we are likely to catastrophise.

These logical errors then affect our surface thinking. We are more likely to be self-critical or tell ourselves everything is hopeless, or tell ourselves that nothing is fair because of the logical errors we make based on our particular core beliefs.

Our core beliefs are built on the basis of a variety of influences. These include our genetic makeup (e.g., an inherited overly reactive nervous system), our experiences (the things that happen to us), the messages we receive (the things people have said to us or the way they have treated us), and the ways we have interpreted these events. If the influences are positive and healthy, our core beliefs tend to be clear, and there are few logical errors. If the influences on us are negative, unhealthy or confusing, our core beliefs tend to be inaccurate, and the logical errors we make are many and strongly influence our automatic thoughts.

Underlying assumptions of logical errors

It has been suggested that each logical error is driven by a specific assumption. If our automatic thoughts are biased, then the biases are driven by our core beliefs and assumptions. Below are some examples of cognitive errors and examples of associated assumptions. Here we are referring to the assumptions that are inevitably made if the errors in our thinking are present.

Table 8: The assumptions underlying each logical error.

Cognitive error	Assumption
Filtering	The only events that matter are failures. I should measure myself by my errors.
Polarised thinking	Everything is always one extreme or the other.
Overgeneralisation	If it's true in one case, it must be true in every case that is even slightly similar.
Jumping to conclusions	If it has always been true in the past, it is going to be true in the future.
Catastrophising	Always think the worst because it is most likely to happen to you.
Personalisation	I am responsible for all bad things, failures, etc.
Control fallacies	You should be able to know in advance what is going to happen. When, after the event, you understand the chain of events that resulted in a bad thing happening, this means that you should have seen the bad thing coming before it happened.
Fallacy of fairness	The world is a fair place, and fairness influences how things turn out.
Blaming	Whether it is me or someone else, someone is always responsible when things are not the way I want them to be.
Shoulds	People have an obligation to do specific things that cannot be avoided.
Emotional reasoning	If a person feels bad, something must be wrong.
Fallacy of change	People must change to meet other people's needs.
Global labelling	A whole person and their entire life can be summed up by a single word (e.g., stupid).
Always being right	People have to choose a side, and there is a right side and a wrong side.

| Heaven's reward fallacy | Choosing to do good things for others will oblige others to do good things in return. |

Let's consider how these logical errors and the assumptions that are made affect automatic thoughts. Consider in this example what this person is saying to herself about her relationship breakdown.

> *I don't know what to do. I can't believe he left. I don't even know what went wrong, but I must have done something... or not done something to cause this to happen* (personalisation). *I should have paid more attention or been kinder... or something* (shoulds). *I am always so hopeless, and I'm never good enough* (global labelling). *It serves me right. I deserve to be in this mess* (blaming). *I have lost everything that is important to me. I should have seen it coming and fixed it before things got this bad* (control fallacy).

Let's break this down and see where this person is making mistakes.

> Without even knowing why the relationship ended, she assumed that she was the one responsible – that there was something she could have done differently to achieve a better outcome (personalisation). It seems unreasonable for her to hold herself responsible when she did not even know why this occurred.

> Again, without knowing what has contributed to the breakdown of the relationship, she comes up with a list of things she should have done, even though she did not know at the time that she was doing anything wrong (shoulds). It is all very well for her to say to herself that she should have done certain things, but we have to assume that if it was obvious that things needed to be done, she would have done them at the time.

> As a result of her version of her contribution to the relationship failing, she is self-critical and attributes certain characteristics to herself that attack her, not just in terms of the relationship problem, but in all things (global labelling). Even if she did make mistakes in her relationship, it does not follow that she is a bad or hopeless person deserving of bad things happening to her.

> Then, even though it was her partner who ended the relationship and without knowing the reasons why the relationship ended, she holds herself responsible and thinks she deserves to have lost something so important to her (blaming). She is pointing the finger at herself before having sufficient information to apportion responsibility.

> Finally, even though she does not understand what happened, she believes she should have acted in a way to prevent her relationship breaking down and ending (control fallacy). This suggests that she should have magically known in advance

what was going to happen and she should have or, indeed, could have controlled the end result.

The errors in this person's thinking have resulted in her feeling much worse than she would have felt if she had not made these errors. Let's find out how to change this way of thinking to protect yourself from the negative effects of logical errors.

Understanding automatic thoughts

The goal here is to teach you to think in a more realistic and balanced way so that you can cope better with the end of your relationship. This is done in a number of steps. Let's start this process.

Everybody experiences automatic thoughts. They reflect our way of making sense of and reacting to the world around us and to internal experiences, such as anxiety or memories and urges. Automatic thoughts are often highly believable, even when they are based on logical errors. As a result of their believability, we tend not to challenge them. If they pass unchallenged, they can have a profound and detrimental effect on our emotional state. For example, if a person thinks they are stupid and they do not challenge that thought, they are likely to feel upset and unworthy.

Consider this example.

> *How could I have been so stupid? I thought things were going ok and then she up and left. I was stupid to believe everything was all right. I was stupid to believe it when she told me she loved me. I was stupid to think our relationship ever meant anything. I was a fool. I am a fool.*

It would be hard to think this way without feeling bad as a consequence. We tend to believe the things we tell ourselves. Even when we do not pay much attention to our self-talk – our running commentary – we can still be affected by it.

Catching automatic thoughts

It is important to pay attention to your automatic thoughts so that their content can be used to identify both the logical errors you are making and, ultimately, your core beliefs. The way to go about this is to keep a thought record related to times when you notice a change in the way you are feeling.

In their simplest form, a thought record asks you to identify the event that has occurred, to take notice of the thoughts that go through your head at the time of the event, and to record the consequences you experience, both in terms of how you feel and how you might act in response. Consider the example below of a simple thought record.

A	B	C
Activating event	Belief or thought	Consequence: emotional and behavioural
Andrew said he was going to come to see me to discuss dividing up our things, but he didn't show up.	I matter so little that he couldn't even be bothered turning up.	I felt so miserable I laid down on my bed and cried on and off for the rest of the evening.
I heard that Andrew went out with two people who used to be friends with both of us and I wasn't invited.	No one likes me. Everyone will choose to be on Andrew's side and not mine.	I felt really down on myself. I sat alone and drank too much.

We do not usually pay much attention to the thoughts that go through our heads, even though they can have such a profound effect on how we are feeling and what we choose to do as a result of feeling that way. To change our thinking, we have to learn to identify our automatic thoughts. When we consider the events that trigger a response in us, we can usually identify what went through our mind at the time.

By keeping track of your automatic thoughts, you can identify patterns in your thinking that are linked with particular negative feelings and the behaviours you choose because you are feeling that way. Use the simple thought record below to keep track of your automatic thoughts in relation to events that stress you.

Simple automatic thoughts worksheet		
A	B	C
Activating event	Belief or thought	Consequence: emotional and behavioural

Worksheet available at elemen.com.au

Understanding and noticing logical errors

Everyone makes logical errors. It is important to understand this point. It is when the error you are making (e.g., everything should be fair) conflicts with how things really are (e.g., the world is neither fair nor unfair; it just is the way it is) that problems arise. However, it is also important to be able to recognise the logical errors you are making so that you can correct them and correct the problems in your core beliefs. To do this, you can try the simple approach of expanding on your thought record form so that you include the types of logical errors that are reflected in your automatic thoughts.

Let's go back to our original thought record form and expand the examples.

Expanded thought record form - Example			
A	B	C	D
Activating event	Belief or thought	Consequence: emotional and behavioural	Logical errors
Andrew said he was going to come to see me to discuss dividing up our things but he didn't show up.	*I matter so little that he couldn't even be bothered turning up.*	*I felt so miserable I laid down on my bed and cried on and off for the rest of the evening.*	*Personalisation*
I heard that Andrew went out with two people who used to be friends with both of us and I wasn't invited.	*No one likes me. Everyone will choose to be on Andrew's side and not mine.*	*I felt really down on myself. I sat alone and drank too much.*	*Overgeneralisation*

In the first example, this person interpreted Andrew's failure to turn up or to let her know that he was not going to be able to make it as an indication that she was unworthy and of little value as a person. She personalised Andrew's rude behaviour. In the second example, she took one instance of Andrew catching up with a couple of friends as evidence that she was losing all her friends. She overgeneralised one incident to all potential incidents.

Below is an expanded thought record form that you can use to identify the logical errors in what you are thinking.

Expanded thought record form			
A	B	C	D
Activating event	Belief or thought	Consequence: emotional and behavioural	Logical errors

Worksheet available at elemen.com.au

Reframing your thoughts (cognitive restructuring)

The process of challenging our negative automatic thoughts is called cognitive restructuring. This is what we are trying to achieve here. The conclusions we reach because of our logical errors should be challenged and replaced with something that is healthier and more accurately reflects how the world really works.

Although there are lots of ways you can go about restructuring your thinking, we are going to introduce you to a straightforward method. We are going to start by ensuring that you understand the difference between fact and opinion. This is important as our thoughts and decision-making should be based on facts and not the opinions we form because of incorrect information that can underlie our core beliefs. For example, an opinion would be "I am stupid". You might form this opinion because someone has repeatedly told you that you are stupid or because they acted in a way that encouraged you to believe you were stupid. It is not the truth or a fact that you are stupid. It is a belief you have or an opinion you have formed because of incorrect information.

We refer to the opinion on which you rely as a work of fiction. That is, you write a story in your head about what is happening and then act as if the story is true. You need to be able to identify when you are relying on the story you have written in your mind rather than basing your thoughts on factual evidence. Let's start by having a go at identifying fact from opinion or fiction. In the spaces provided, you can add other things you have been thinking and consider whether they are facts or opinions.

Fact or fiction worksheet		
Statement	*Fact*	*Fiction*
I am stupid		√
I love bushwalking	√	
I am ugly		
I forgot to renew my driver's licence		
No one likes me		
This will be a disaster		
I'm not good enough		
I am single		
I will never fall in love again		
I hate my job		
I should have known what was about to happen		
There are times when people feel stressed		

Worksheet available at elemen.com.au

The facts here are:

> I love bushwalking
>
> I forgot to renew my driver's licence
>
> I am single
>
> I hate my job
>
> There are times when people feel stressed

The statements that are opinions are:

> I am stupid
>
> I am ugly
>
> No one likes me
>
> This will be a disaster
>
> I'm not good enough
>
> I will never fall in love again
>
> I should have known what was about to happen

Why should we make this distinction between what is a fact and what is an opinion? It is because the errors in thinking we make are based on opinion and not on fact. Further, because we hold this opinion, we assume that it is true because we are thinking it and not because it is based on fact.

To tidy up our thinking and remove the logical errors, we have to rely on those thoughts that are based on fact alone. We can reject thoughts that are just based on our opinion because our opinions can be faulty. Factual information will be a good guide for us to determine whether or not we should believe what we are thinking.

Cognitive restructuring worksheet - Example
What I am thinking *I am thinking that no one likes me and that everyone will choose Andrew's side so I will have no friends.*
Facts supporting the thought *Andrew did catch up with two of our friends, and I wasn't invited (although I don't know the circumstances of that invitation).*
Facts contradicting the thought *Andrew only caught up with these people on one occasion without me.* *These people have not indicated they do not wish to be friends with me.* *Other friends have invited me out on lots of occasions without Andrew.* *Friends have offered me lots of support.*
Is this thought based on factual evidence or opinion? *This thought that no one would like me and I would lose all my friends is just an opinion I formed because I was hurt that Andrew went out with two of our friends. This opinion doesn't take into account all my other friends and all the times I have been invited to join them on various outings and get-togethers.*

By looking at the facts for and against a point of view being true, you can work out the value of holding that opinion. It seems like a waste of time to be thinking a particular thing and being negatively affected by it emotionally and behaviourally if you cannot even determine that the opinion reflects the truth. You can use the worksheet below to examine your thoughts in terms of the facts supporting what you are thinking and the facts that contradict what you are thinking.

Cognitive restructuring worksheet
What I am thinking
Facts supporting the thought
Facts contradicting the thought
Is this thought based on factual evidence or opinion?

Worksheet available at elemen.com.au

Rather than looking at facts for and against the truth of your thoughts, another very easy approach to reframing your thinking is what is called compassionate cognitive restructuring. Here, you are asked to look at your thoughts in a more compassionate way. Ask yourself what you would say to a person who was in a similar situation to you. In all likelihood, you would say something much kinder and closer to the truth than you are saying to yourself.

Consider this example.

Example	
Your friend says:	*No one will ever want me. I will never be in another relationship.*
You might say:	*That's not true. You have so much to give to a relationship. You are loyal and loving. Why would someone not want that in a partner?*

It is the case that we often are harder on ourselves than others think is necessary. We set higher standards. For example, you might say that you should never make a mistake and call yourself stupid if you do. Your friend would say that everyone makes mistakes and all we can do is learn from them.

It is interesting that, although you trust your good friends, you choose not to believe them when they make an honest, positive statement about you. Remember how it feels when the reverse occurs when you make a positive statement to your friend, and they dismiss what you say or reject it in favour of a statement you see as false. It is frustrating. You can be as kind and supportive to yourself as you are to the people you care about.

Making the restructured thinking habitual

To get to a point where you are thinking in a healthier way, you need to go through a process of deliberately challenging your thinking. You need to overlearn noticing your automatic thoughts and then reframing them into a healthier and more accurate alternative thought. You will then challenge your thinking and adjust your automatic thoughts without giving it much attention. Eventually, you will not even have to do that because your core beliefs will be corrected to offer you a more accurate template of how the world works and how you fit into that world. 'Practice makes perfect' – or in a cognitive restructured way, 'Practice makes adequate for the demands of the situation'!

Targeting the assumptions

Let's not forget about those assumptions that underlie the errors you make in your thinking. We need to challenge those assumptions to completely correct our thinking. Remember, if the assumptions that underlie the error are shown to be wrong, there is every reason to abandon the logical error and replace it with a more logical point of view.

There are a few ways you can challenge the assumptions that underlie logical errors. We are going to focus on three approaches. Firstly, we are going to apply the strategy of looking at the advantages and disadvantages of holding an assumption. Consider the following example of someone who is predicting that things are going to work out poorly.

Assumption worksheet: Advantages and disadvantages
Logical error and assumptions *Catastrophising. Always think the worst because it is most likely to happen to you.*
Advantages *I will always be on 'red alert' in case something happens.*
Disadvantages *I will be on 'red alert' all the time, even when it is not necessary for me to be so.* *I will find it hard to feel any joy about anything if I constantly worry about everything going wrong.* *I will waste a lot of time worrying about things that end up not being as bad as I thought they were going to be.*

Challenging the assumption that underlies a tendency to catastrophise, you can see that there are many more disadvantages to doing this than there are advantages. In fact, experiencing the disadvantages may turn out to be worse than the possible thing in the future you are worrying about.

Secondly, you can act against the assumptions. What would happen if the assumption was incorrect? Consider the following example.

Assumption worksheet: Acting against the assumption
Logical error and assumptions *Catastrophising. Always think the worst because it is most likely to happen to you.*
Things that might happen if I acted like the assumption was not true *I might be able to relax and feel calmer.* *I might find some enjoyment in the things I do.* *I might experience some peace of mind.* *I might look forward to some things in the future.*

By acting as if the assumption is false, you can usually identify the positive things that would occur as a consequence. All of these things are better than predicting a gloomy future. Remember, spending your time thinking about how badly things are likely to turn out in the future also removes all the pleasure from the present.

Finally, you can argue against the assumption. You can take the perspective that the assumption is wrong and develop an argument for your case. Consider the following example.

Assumption worksheet: Arguing against the assumption
Logical error and assumptions *Catastrophising. Always think the worst because it is most likely to happen to you.*
Arguments against the assumption *Thinking something might happen will not make it happen.* *There is no cosmic force that is directing all bad things my way.*

Here, you are thinking of the *facts* that can be used to present a good argument that the assumption associated with the logical error is not accurate. This will allow you to challenge your error-ridden thinking and replace it with healthier thinking that will not encourage you to feel strong, negative emotions.

Below is a worksheet you can use to challenge the assumptions that underlie your errors in thinking.

Targeting assumptions worksheet
Logical error and assumption
Advantages
Disadvantages
Things that might happen if I acted like the assumption was not true
Arguments against the assumption

Worksheet is available at elemen.com.au

Here, we have asked you to consider challenging the sorts of thoughts you might have that are likely to make you feel worse than you would otherwise feel if you did not think that way. You have learned to access these logical errors by paying attention to your automatic thoughts that serve as the running commentary your mind provides. You have learned ways to challenge these errors and remove them and their influence from your thinking. The goal of doing these things has been to help you manage your distress and protect yourself from being upset in the future.

Assertive communication

Another useful focus of our attention is on assertive communication. We need to consider your assertiveness skills because you are likely to be faced with many challenging interactions that occur at the time of a relationship breakdown. These may include personal issues, such as the future of the relationship, or more practical things, such as living arrangements, property settlements or, importantly, parenting arrangements if you have children.

Assertiveness refers to standing up for your rights without trampling over the rights of others. Some people mistake assertiveness for aggressiveness which refers to the aggressive assertion of your rights irrespective of the rights of others. At the other extreme is passivity where a person will not stand up for their own rights and allow others to walk over them.

So, the aim here is to teach you to stand up for your own rights without trampling over the rights of other people. An assertive interpersonal style will allow you to negotiate for what you want without demanding that it happen.

Asking for change

Firstly, we need to consider how to assertively solve problems by making reasonable requests for change or appropriate requests for what you would like to have happen. Many people find this difficult. They will start to make a request but are easily derailed by the deflection techniques used by the other person. Alternatively, they will start to make a request but are then affected by the annoyance you feel about the response of the other person. This following step-by-step guide is designed to help you plan ahead for how you are going to manage a request for change.

Define the problem situation

You should start by defining the problem you are facing. Do this by focusing on the facts of the matter and not your interpretation of the situation. You should do this by being as specific as possible. Avoid generalisations like "It's always the case…" or "Nothing ever goes right…". So, keep a narrow focus on the situation you have identified that you wish to change. Limit this to one problem at a time rather than bombarding the other person with a list of grievances.

> *Despite my repeated requests for you to make arrangements for me or someone in my family to collect my belongings, this has not occurred.*

Describe how you are feeling

Here, you get a chance to describe how you feel about the situation. Remember, you are referring to how you feel and not how someone else *made* you feel. Be clear about the link between your feelings and the problem situation. Again, do not generalise to all situations or all problems.

Avoid blaming others. By blaming others, you put them on the defensive and little is ever resolved as a consequence. When you talk about how you are feeling, use what is called an 'I message'. That is, your descriptions of your feelings should start with something like "I feel…". No one can argue with you about this matter. They cannot say that you do not feel something that you have stated you feel. If you started with "You make me feel…", it is likely the other person would argue that it was not their intention to make you feel that way, and if you do, that is your problem. Using 'I messages' allows you to avoid all of this discussion. In any case, you are the person who decides how you feel, and you should be able to relate that feeling to the other person.

This is a good opportunity to express your feelings. It is a mistake to assume that others know what you are thinking or feeling if you have not said so. If you have not said how you feel, the other person can do little more than guess. We make a mistake by assuming that someone who knows you well can 'mindread' and automatically know what you are thinking or feeling. Clear communication works much better than allowing others to guess.

> *I am disappointed that this arrangement hasn't been made and annoyed it has gone on for so long.*

Make your request for change

Here, you should make a statement about what you want to happen. You need to be brief. Do not turn your request into a lecture. Also, you need to be specific. Clearly state what you want rather than use terms that are not concrete. For example, it will not help to say, "I want things to improve" because that is a generalised statement that can be interpreted in a multitude of ways. You would be better off saying, "I want you to remove your name from the lease" or "I want you to remove your things from the house by the end of a fortnight".

> *I want an arrangement made for me or one of my family members to collect my belongings this weekend, on either Saturday or Sunday.*

Outline possible positive consequences

If the other person initially does not want to agree with your request for change, you may choose to point out the positive consequences that would follow from the agreement. Do not make wild promises. Just focus on the positive things that are likely to happen from the change you are requesting. You are building the argument for what you want. For example, you could say, "I want you to remove your name from the lease. If you do this, you will no longer be held liable for rent payments".

> *If I, or a family member, can collect my belongings this weekend, I will make no claim on household items that we jointly purchased.*

Outline potential negative consequences

If the other person is still reluctant to agree with what you are asking, you can outline the likely negative consequences for them if they choose not to comply with your wishes. Do not threaten. Simply state what you understand to be the bad things that will happen if things do not change. For example, you could say, "I want you to remove your things from the house by the end of a fortnight. If you do not, I will move your things into the garage where it is damp and they might be affected".

It is important to remember that you should only outline negative consequences that you are certain you are willing to follow through on. You, too, have to live with the negative consequences, so do not outline something you are not willing to do or have to happen.

> *If I am prevented from collecting my belongings because you fail to make an arrangement for me or a family member to do so, I will seek the assistance of the police to safely remove my possessions and I will pursue settlement regarding jointly purchased household items.*

So, to summarise, when making a request for change, do the following:

    Define the problem situation

    Describe how you are feeling

    Make your request for change

    Outline possible positive consequences

    Outline potential negative consequences

This is a good approach to standing up for your rights in an assertive manner. It is relatively simple and straightforward. You can also work out in advance what it is you want to say and this protects you from having to make it up on the spot.

However, standing up for your rights may not be enough in itself if you are aiming for assertive communication. You need to be able to negotiate for what you want with a person who may be inclined not to give this to you. Consider the following negotiation process.

Negotiating for what you want

To negotiate with another person, your starting point needs to be that you both have needs that are equally important. This will require some effort on your part. It is easy for us to assume that what we want is right and what the other person wants is wrong. However, if you hold this view, then any interaction about the issue in question will be an argument rather than a negotiation.

There are six steps that should be taken when you enter into a negotiation. Let's consider each of these steps.

Know what it is you want

Know what it is that you are negotiating for. You must have a clearly defined goal if you are to enter into a negotiation. If you are not clear about what you want then how can the other person have any idea?

Make a statement of what you want in specific terms

In specific terms and being as clear as possible, make a statement about what you want or do not want to have happen. This can be in terms of what you want or do not want the other person to do. However, it may also be in terms of what you want as the outcome.

Listen to the point of view of the other person

Your goal here is to understand the other person's perspective. To do this, you have to listen carefully to what the other person has to say about their point of view. You should use active listening skills where you can ask for clarification or elaboration rather than passively listen. Remember, you may not agree with the other person's perspective. What you should be doing is appreciating that they have a point of view that might be different from yours, but it is their point of view nonetheless.

Make a proposal

Next, you should make a proposal that offers a resolution. The proposal should not be solely based on what you want. It should take into account the other person's needs. This can be a challenging step that may take some thought on your part. It is easier to conceptualise a proposal that takes into account what both of you want if you approach it with the goal of achieving a 'win-win' outcome. This is where you get some of what you want, and the other person gets some of what they want. A win-win proposal has a much better chance of being accepted than a 'my way or the highway' approach.

Ask for a counterproposal

If your proposal is not accepted, do not be disheartened. Ask the other person for a counterproposal. Remember that your goal is to reach a point where you can both accept the proposal, even if you both do not get all of what you want.

Aim for compromise

The end result of any negotiation is typically a compromise. You are unlikely to get everything your way, but neither is the other person. You are aiming to reach a middle point that is satisfactory to you both. There are a variety of ways a compromise can be achieved:

> You give up some of what you want to gain some of what you want, and so does the other person.

> You might split the difference.

> You might agree that you do it your way when you are in control, and the other person does it their way when they are in control.

This last type of compromise can be useful when people cannot agree with parenting rules. In these cases, you might decide that you make the rules when the children are with you, and the other parent makes the rules when the children are with them, as long as the children are safe.

Often at the end of a relationship there are issues that will have to be negotiated. You need to feel able to stand up for your rights and you need to be able to negotiate for an acceptable outcome.

Improving the quality of your life

As stated, this is a difficult time in your life. You have to move from a position where you have taken your partner's needs into consideration to one where you can choose what you do. This can feel a bit like being set adrift. For example, not having to tell someone where you are going or when you will return can feel very unsettling.

One thing that can happen as a result of spending a long time accommodating someone else's needs is that you lose sight of the things that you can do to please yourself. It is important that you have the opportunity to do some things for yourself. Having a balance between the tasks that are important that you must undertake and some leisure time will improve the balance of your life.

It is important that you choose activities that are meaningful to you and that will improve the satisfaction you feel with your life. It is easy to fill your life with things to do, even leisure activities. However, not all of these potential activities will give you a sense of satisfaction. This is because not all activities are important to you. You should choose activities that are of high value to you if your goal is to make your life fuller *and* more meaningful.

How do you know what activities would contribute the most to improving the quality of your life? We often do not think about what we value as we go through our busy day and the question of what a person values can often be confusing to them. Borrowing from a particular therapy called Acceptance and Commitment Therapy, we have included here an exercise in values clarification that will help you decide which activities would be of the greatest value to you.

The goal of this exercise is to identify ways you can add to your life the things that you value the most. The purpose of doing this is to improve your quality of life by having more things in your life that matter to you the most.

When we refer to the things we value, we are not referring to a specific activity. For example, you may have a value related to spending more time with your family. A specific activity that might flow from this value is to have a meal with your family once a week.

Below is a diagram that contains labels for various life domains. A life domain is an area of your life that reflects one portion of who you are and what you do. This is an example of what we are talking about when we refer to your life domain map.

Values clarification exercise for choosing preferred activities

Step 1 involves you listing as many life domains as you can think of that are relevant to you. We have included some life domains that people often list, but feel free to change them and add new ones that reflect your life. What you are doing here is building your life domain map. Take your time to think up as many life domains as you understand to be part of your life. Other examples might be travel, exercise, etc.

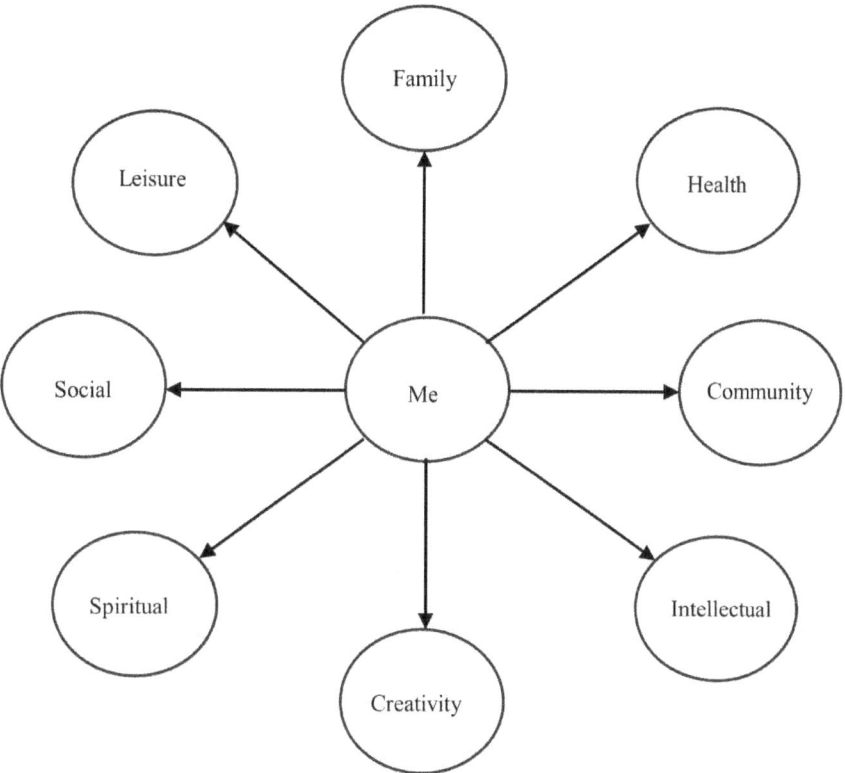

Figure 7: Example of a life domain map.

Step 2 involves you identifying what you already have in your life for the various life domains. Remember, list the values you have (e.g., ample time with your family) rather than specific activities (e.g., Sunday lunch with your family). You will begin to notice that some domains in your life have received lots of attention, but other domains have received little or no attention. Here is an example of the types of values that might appear in the family domain.

    Family domain:

        Time with family

        Special time with individual family members

        Spending time with the young members of my family

        Important family gatherings

Remember, you are listing here what you already have of value in your life with regard to this domain. This is not a list of the things you would like to have available to you.

Step 3 involves you now considering the things you would like to have in your life in each of the domains. Again, focus on the values (e.g., more quality time with my parents) rather than activities (e.g., visiting my parents on Sunday afternoons).

At this point, you will begin to notice several things.

> You will see that there are domains of your life that receive lots of attention already and you want very little else in that domain. Things in these domains are already satisfactory so there is limited purpose in focusing your attention on them.

> You will see that there are domains of your life where you have very little but you also do not really want very much more. These do not deserve your attention either.

> Importantly, you will see there are domains of your life where you have very little, and there are many things that you want in that domain that you do not already have available to you. Focusing your attention on these would give you the greatest benefit.

It is the third type of life domain that will become the focus of attention from here on. This is because this focus will have the greatest chance of having the most important impact on the quality of your life.

Step 4 involves focusing on those life domains where you do not have enough of what matters to you, and there is very much more that you want to include in your life. In this step, you should consider how those values that you want to put into your life might translate into specific activities. It is here that the 'what to do' component of the exercise occurs. For example, if you have a value associated with spending more time with your family, you might now consider ways that could happen by identifying specific activities you could engage in that would bring that value into your life (e.g., arranging family get-togethers, organising an online shared family photo site where family members can post photos for all family members to see).

Step 5 involves identifying any barriers that might prevent you from engaging in these activities that would bring the things that you value into your life and finding ways around these barriers. For example, you may not be able to catch up in person with family members if they live in places distant from you, but you could overcome this barrier by arranging Skype or Zoom get-togethers.

Of course, there will be things you want that are of value to you that you just cannot have because of real limitations. For example, you may like to travel, but you cannot do so because you cannot afford the expense. However, if travel is of high value, then the quality of your life might be enhanced by spending time exploring places online or watching travel documentaries. Although not exactly what you would give the highest value, these activities are still related to the thing that matters to you.

Remember that your goal is to introduce activities that are of high value to you that will improve the quality of your life. If you are going to devote the time to engaging in these types of activities, it will matter that you focus on the activities that are associated with your highest values.

Looking after yourself

During this difficult time, you need to look after yourself. Briefly, here are some things you might like to consider.

> The end of a relationship is a difficult time, and you can expect to feel bad for a while. Do not criticise yourself for feeling this way or expect yourself to act like this is not a stressful period in your life.
>
> Recognise that your thinking will be affected by your distress. It will be harder for you to think clearly about things and harder for you to make decisions. Do not put undue pressure on yourself.
>
> Look after your needs. Do not expect too much of yourself. The distress you feel and the sleepless nights you have can wear you out. Keep that in mind and do not expect yourself to be functioning in top form. Remember that even if you are functioning at, say, 60 percent of which you are capable, you are still doing the best you can at that moment in time.
>
> Identify what you might need from others and seek it out. This might be support or companionship. You might turn to others for advice. Do not feel bad about turning to others for help. In all likelihood, you would offer help to others if they were in the same situation as you.
>
> Know, with absolute certainty, that you will not continue to feel this way forever. You will be able to move on with your life without feeling distressed. You are taking this moment in time to adjust to what has happened.

It is also worth keeping in mind that even things that feel overwhelmingly distressing can have a good outcome. We know that these types of events in our lives can cause us to change the way we look at things and reprioritise the things that are important to us. In this way, your outlook on life can change as a consequence of distressing events. You need to get past this difficult stage in your reaction to what has happened to reach the point where this change can occur.

We wish you the best for the future.

Additional reading

Clark, D.A., & Beck, A.T. (2012). *The anxiety and worry workbook: The cognitive behavioral solution.* New York: The Guilford Press.

Doka, K.J. (Ed.). (1989). *Disenfranchised grief: Recognizing hidden sorrow.* US: Lexington Books.

Tobin, D., Holroyd, K., Reynolds, R., & Wigal, J.K. (1989). The hierarchical structure of the Coping Strategies Inventory. *Cognitive Therapy and Research, 13(4),* 343-361.

Eifer, G.H., Forsyth, J.P., & Hayes, S.C. (2005). *Acceptance and commitment therapy for anxiety disorders.* New York: New Harbinger Publications.